How to Assess Program Implementation

Jean A. King
Lynn Lyons Morris
Carol Taylor Fitz-Gibbon

Center for the Study of Evaluation
University of California, Los Angeles

SAGE PUBLICATIONS
The International Professional Publishers
Newbury Park   London   New Delhi

The second edition of the *Program Evaluation Kit* was developed at the Center for the Study of Evaluation, Graduate School of Education, University of California, Los Angeles.

The development of this second edition of the CSE *Program Evaluation Kit* was supported in part by a grant from the National Institute of Education, currently known as the Office of Educational Research and Improvement. However, the opinions expressed herein do not necessarily reflect the position or policy of that agency and no official endorsement should be inferred.

The second edition of the *Program Evaluation Kit* is published and distributed by Sage Publications, Inc., Newbury Park, California, under an exclusive agreement with The Regents of the University of California.

For information address:

SAGE Publications, Inc.
2455 Teller Road
Newbury Park, California 91320

SAGE Publications Ltd.
6 Bonhill Street
London EC2A 4PU
United Kingdom

SAGE Publications India Pvt. Ltd.
M-32 Market
Greater Kailash I
New Delhi 110 048 India

Printed in the United States of America

Library of Congress Cataloging-in-Publication Data

King, Jean A.
    How to assess program implementation / Jean A. King, Lynn Lyons
Morris, Carol Taylor Fitz-Gibbons.
        p. cm.
    Bibliography: p.
    Includes index.
    ISBN 0-8039-3130-1 (pbk.)
    1. Evaluation research (Social action programs)   I. Morris, Lynn
Lyons.   II. Fitz-Gibbons, Carol Taylor.   III. Title.
H61.K545   1987
361.6′1′068--dc19   87-21645
                    CIP

92 93 94 10

Contents

Author's Note

When I took on the task of revising *How to Measure Program Implementation*, little did I realize the challenges of updating someone else's finished product, particularly one that I respected and had found helpful. Several individuals were vital to my being able to complete the project. First, for my early introduction to the evaluation field, I must thank Jason Millman, who taught me that real evaluators don't have to drink coffee. Second, while I am unable to name specifically the numerous people and projects I have worked with in a decade of evaluations, as a group they provided me the insights and examples that appear here. In addition, the thoughtful editorial assistance of Joan Herman was critical to sustaining my revision efforts, as was the excellent word processing of Janice Sayas, often on a moment's notice. Finally, as ever, my family—Stuart, Ben, and Hannah—both inspired my work and put up with me throughout the experience, for which I thank them. I at last have the sense that this project really may be completed.

Jean A. King
New Orleans, LA

Acknowledgments

The preparation of this second edition of the Center for the Study of Evaluation *Program Evaluation Kit* has been a challenging task, made possible only through the combined efforts of a number of individuals.

First and foremost, Drs. Lynn Lyons Morris and Carol Taylor Fitz-Gibbon, the authors and editor of the original Kit. Together, they authored all eight of the original volumes, an enormous undertaking that required incredible knowledge, dedication, persistence, and painstaking effort. Lynn also worked relentlessly as editor of the entire set. Having struggled through only a revision, I stand in great awe of Lynn's and Carol's enormous accomplishment. This second edition retains much of their work and obviously would not have been possible without them.

Thanks also are due to Gene V Glass, Ernie House, Michael Q. Patton, Carol Weiss, and Robert Boruch, who reviewed our plans and offered specific assistance in targeting needed revisions. The work would not have proceeded without Marvin C. Alkin, who planted the seeds for the second edition and collaborated very closely during the initial planning phases.

I would like to acknowledge especially the contribution and help of Michael Q. Patton. True to form, Michael was an excellent, utilization-focused formative evaluator for the final draft manuscript, carefully responding to our work and offering innumerable specific suggestions for its improvement. We have incorporated into the *Handbook* his framework for differentiating among kinds of evaluation studies (formative, summative, implementation, outcomes).

Many staff members at the Center for the Study of Evaluation contributed to the production of the Kit. The entire effort was supervised by Aeri Lee, able office manager at the Center. Katherine Fry, word processing expert, was able to accomplish incredible graphic feats for the *Handbook* and tirelessly labored on manuscript production and data transfer. Ruth Paysen, who was a major contributor to the production of the original Kit, also was a painstaking and dedicated proofreader for the second edition. Margie Franco, Tori Gouveia, and Katherine Lu also participated in the production effort.

Marie Freeman and Pamela Aschbacher, also from the Center, contributed their ideas, editorial skills, and endless examples. Carli

Rogers, of UCLA Contracts and Grants, was both caring and careful in her negotiations for us.

At Sage Publications, thanks to Sara McCune for her encouragement and to Mitch Allen for his nudging and patience.

And at the Center for the Study of Evaluation, the project surely would not have been possible without Eva L. Baker, Director. Eva is a continuing source of encouragement, ideas, support, fun, and friendship.

—Joan L. Herman
Center for the Study of Evaluation
University of California, Los Angeles

Chapter 1

Assessing Program Implementation: An Overview

How to Assess Program Implementation is one component of the *Program Evaluation Kit,* a set of guidebooks written primarily for people who have been assigned the role of program evaluator. The evaluator has the often challenging job of scrutinizing and describing programs so that people may judge the program's quality as it stands or determine ways to make it better. Evaluation almost always demands gathering and analyzing information about a program's status and sharing it in one form or another with program planners, staff, or funders.

This book deals with the task of describing a program's *implementation*—that is, how the program looks in operation.[1] Keeping track of what the program looks like in actual practice is one of your major responsibilities as a program evaluator because you cannot evaluate something well without first describing what that something is. If you have taken on an evaluation project, therefore, you will need to produce a description of the program that is sufficiently detailed to enable those who will use the evaluation results to act wisely. This description may or may not be written. Even if delivered informally, however, it should highlight the program's most important characteristics, including a description of the context in which the program exists—its setting and participants—as well as its distinguishing activities and materials. The implementation report should also include varying amounts of backup data to support the accuracy of the description.

The overall objective of this book is to help you develop skills to plan an evaluation of a program implementation and to design and use appropriate instruments for generating data to support your description.

The guidelines in the book derive from three sources: the experience of evaluators at the Center for the Study of Evaluation, University of California, Los Angeles; advice from experts in the fields of educational measurement and evaluation; and comments of people in school, system, and state settings who used a field test edition of the book. *How to Assess Program Implementation* has three specific purposes:

(1) to provide a rationale for describing program implementation;
(2) to help you plan an implementation evaluation that is both workable and useful to decision makers; and
(3) to guide you in designing instruments to produce supporting data so that you can assure yourself and your audience that your description is accurate.

The book has seven chapters and an appendix. Chapter 1 presents a rationale for examining a program's implementation. Chapter 2 provides initial questions to assist in planning an implementation evaluation. Chapters 3 through 6 constitute the "how to assess" section of the book. Chapter 3 discusses how to plan an implementation evaluation, followed by three methods chapters (Chapters 4, 5, and 6) devoted to the examination of existing records, self-report measures (questionnaires and interviews), and observation techniques. Chapter 7 addresses data analysis, summary, and reporting issues. The appendix gives a list of questions that an implementation evaluation report might answer.

Wherever possible, procedures in the "how to" sections are presented step-by-step to give you maximum practical advice with minimum theoretical interference. Many of the recommended procedures, however, are methods for measuring program implementation under ideal circumstances. It is no surprise that few evaluation situations in the real world match the ideal, and, because of this, the goal of the evaluator should be to provide the best information *possible. You should not expect, therefore, to duplicate the suggestions in this book step-by-step.* What you *can* do is to examine the principles and examples provided and then adapt them to your situation, whatever the evaluation constraints, data requirements, and report needs. This means gathering the most credible information allowable in your circumstances and presenting the conclusions so as to make them most useful to the evaluation's clients or primary users.

The clients are the people or groups who need information from an evaluation for a distinct purpose. You can serve clients in a number of ways, from merely conducting the studies they sponsor to actively collaborating with them in deciding first what to study and then what to do with the results. In any event, you should remember that every evaluation can potentially be of use to many individuals, each of whom may have different information needs and different criteria for what is considered believable information. Given your situation, your job is to do the best evaluation you possibly can.

Why Look at Program Implementation?

An important function of most evaluations is answering the question, Does the combination of materials, activities, and administrative arrangements that constitute this program seem to lead to the achievement of its objectives? In the course of an evaluation, evaluators appropriately devote time and energy to measuring the *attitudes* and *achievement* of program participants. Such a focus reflects a decision to judge program effectiveness by looking at *outcomes* and asking such questions as the following: To what extent were stated program objectives attained? What other results did that program produce? How well did the participants do? Was there support for what went on in the program? Most evaluations consider such questions.

But to consider *only* questions of program outcomes may limit the usefulness of an evaluation. Suppose evaluation data suggest emphatically that the program was a success. You can say, "It worked!" But unless you have taken care to describe the details of the program's operations, you may be unable to answer a question that logically follows such a judgment of success: "*What* worked?" If you cannot answer that, you will have wasted effort measuring the outcomes of events that cannot be described and therefore remain a mystery. Unless the programmatic black box is opened and its activities made explicit, the evaluation may be unable to identify strengths or suggest appropriate changes.

If this happens to you, you will not be alone. As a matter of fact, you will be in good company. Few evaluation reports pay enough attention to describing the processes of a program that helped participants achieve its outcomes. Some reports assume, for example, that mentioning the title and the funding source of the project provides sufficient description of program events. Other reports devote pages to tables of data (e.g., "Types of Students Participating" or "Teachers Receiving In-Service Training by Subject Matter Area") on the assumption that these data will adequately describe the program processes for the reader. Some reports may provide a short but inadequate description of the program's major features (e.g., materials developed or purchased, instructor and student in-class activities, employment of aides, administrative support, or provisions for special training). After reading the description, the reader may still be left with only a vague notion of how often or for what duration particular activities occurred or how program features affected daily life at the program sites.

To compound the problem of missing or insufficient description, evaluation reports seldom tell where and how evaluators obtained information about program implementation. If the information came from the most typical sources—the project proposal and conversations with project personnel—then the report should describe the efforts made to determine whether the program described in the proposal or during conversations matched the program that actually occurred. Few evaluations give a clear picture of what the program that took place actually looked like and, among those that do, most do not pay enough attention to verifying that the picture is an accurate one. Corroborating data from a variety of sources are valuable for two reasons: (1) because they fill in what may be incomplete pictures; and (2) because they provide support for what may be controversial claims.

It could be argued that some lack of attention to detail and accuracy is justifiable in situations where no one wants to know about the exact features of the program. This, however, is a false argument because you simply cannot interpret a program's results without knowing the details of its implementation. For one thing, an evaluation that ignores implementation will combine results from places where the program was conscientiously installed with those from sites that may have decided "let's not and say we did." If achievement or attitude results from the overall evaluation are discouraging, then what is to be done? This scenario typifies a poor evaluation study, but unfortunately, it describes many large-scale program evaluations from the 1970s, including a few of those most notorious for showing "no effect" in expensive federal programs (e.g., the 1970 evaluation of Project Follow-Through).

What is more, ignoring implementation—even when a thorough program description is not explicitly required—means that information has been lost. This information, if properly collected, interpreted, and presented, can provide present and future audiences a picture of what good or poor programs look like. One important function of an evaluation report is to serve as a program record. Without such documentation educators may continue to duplicate the mistakes of the past.

Why, then, look at program implementation? A thorough description of what happened during program implementation can provide program staff and other interested parties information about which program features worked and which did not. At the same time such a description creates a historical record of the program that may be of value to others who want to implement it or a similar program, particularly when the program itself no longer exists. The appropriate question to ask is not *why* look at program implementation but, rather, *why not?* Given the ongoing value of the results of such an evaluation, evaluators would be remiss not to provide as much implementation information as they can.

By now, two points should be clear:

— Description, in as much detail as possible, of the materials, activities, processes, and administrative arrangements that characterize a particular program is an important part of its evaluation.
— An adequate description of a program, including supporting data from different sources, helps to ensure the thoroughness and accuracy of an evaluation.

How much attention *you* choose to give to implementation in your own situation will substantially affect the quality of your evaluation. A detailed implementation report intended for people unfamiliar with the program should include attention to program characteristics and supporting data, as described in Table 1.

A glance at the possible questions for an implementation evaluation listed in the Appendix suggests that assembling information and writing a detailed implementation report about even a small program can be a nearly impossible task for one person working within the constraints of a typical evaluation. To help you in such a situation, the remainder of this chapter poses two basic questions to consider as you begin to plan your implementation evaluation. Careful attention to these questions prior to the formal planning stage will help ensure that you understand the exact purpose of your evaluation and, in a general sense, the type of data collection methods you want to consider.

**Question 1. What Purpose Will
Your Implementation Study Serve?**

This question asks you to consider your role with regard to the program. Your role is primarily determined by the *use* to which the implementation information you supply will be put. The question of use will override any other you may ask about program implementation.

TABLE 1
Topics Covered by a Thorough Implementation Report

Descriptions of Program Characteristics

Background and contextual information about the program. For example, the place of origin of the program; the nature of the program sites—their demographic characteristics and political atmosphere; the breadth of participation per site; how need for the program was determined; the relationship between the program chosen or designed and the goals and objectives of its constituency; the historical background of the program; its target student group; the background, qualifications, and activities of program personnel; administrative features.

Critical features of the program. For example, the budget for program implementation; what materials are used and how they have been selected or developed; the physical setting of instruction; student activities; grouping of students for instructional purposes; teacher-pupil ratio; teacher preparation for program; schedule of program activities; the level of parent and community involvement; overall program rationale.

Analyses and Discussion of Results

Implementation measures. For example, representativeness of program features discussed; reason for selection of a program feature for examination; methods and bases of instrument development or selection; qualifications of instrument administrators; quality and limitations of the measures used; data collection procedures.

Discussion of program implementation. For example, amount of program life covered by the report; if there is a comparison group, the kinds and degree of differences and similarities between the two groups and the programs they are receiving; kinds of decisions made, by whom; degree of program variation; the "typical" program experience; future program development and/or evaluation.

If you have responsibility for producing a *summary statement* about the general effectiveness of the program, then you will probably report to a funding agency, a government office, or some other representative of the program's constituency. You may be expected to describe the program, to produce a statement concerning the achievement of its intended goals, to note unanticipated outcomes, and possibly to make comparisons with an alternative program. If these tasks resemble the features of your job, you will assume the role of *summative* evaluator.

On the other hand, your evaluation task may characterize you as a *helper* and *advisor* to program planners and developers. During the early stages of the program's operations—or even late in its life—you may be called on to describe and monitor program activities, to test periodically for progress toward achievement or attitude change, to look for potential problems, and to identify areas where the program needs to be augmented, modified, or improved. You may or may not be required to produce a formal report at the end of your activities. In this situation, you are a troubleshooter and a problem solver, a person whose overall task may not be clearly defined. If these more loosely defined tasks resemble the features of your job, you are a *formative* evaluator. Sometimes an evaluator is asked to assume both roles simultaneously—a difficult and hectic assignment, but one that usually is possible.

While concerns of both the formative and summative evaluator focus on collecting information and reporting to appropriate groups, the assessment and description of program implementation within each evaluation role varies greatly—so greatly in fact than different names are used to characterize the two kinds of implementation focus. Description of program implementation for summative evaluation is often called *program documentation*. A documentation of a program is its official description outlining the fixed critical features of the program as well as diverse variations that planners may have allowed. Documentation connotes something well-defined and solid. Documentation of a program—its summative evaluation—should occur only after the program has had sufficient time to correct its initial problems and function smoothly.

On the other hand, description of program implementation for formative evaluation can be called *program monitoring* or *evaluation for program improvement*. Monitoring is a more active, less fixed process than documentation. The more fluid nature of monitoring reflects the evolving nature of the program and its formative evaluation requirements. The formative evaluator's job is not only to describe the program, but also to keep vigilant watch over its development and to call to the attention of program staff what is happening. Program monitoring in formative evaluation should in part reveal to what extent the program as implemented matches what its planners intended and should also provide a basis for deciding whether parts of the program ought to be improved, replaced, or augmented. Formative evaluation occurs while the program is still developing and can be modified on the basis of evaluation findings.

Assessing implementation for program documentation

Part of the task of the summative evaluator is to record, for external distribution, an official description of what the program looked like in operation. This program documentation may be used for the following purposes: accountability, creating a lasting description of the program, and providing a list of the possible causes of a program's effects.

(1) Accountability. In most cases, program staff will be accountable for documenting the implementation of intended program features. In other words, they will need to show how the money allocated for the program has been spent. This role of program documentation has been called the *signal function,* providing an external agency with a sign of compliance typically in the form of a report saying "We did everything we said we were going to do." While some may demean this type of evaluation, its successful and timely completion is often critical to continued funding, and its importance should not be underestimated.

While basic, the signal function is not the only role for accountability in implementation evaluations. Sometimes the expected outcomes of a program, such as heightened independence or creativity among learners, are intangible and difficult to measure. At other times program outcomes may be remote and occur at some time in the future, after the program has concluded and its participants have moved on. This kind of outcome—concerned with, for instance, such matters as responsible citizenship, success on the job, or reduced recidivism—cannot be achieved by the participants during the program. Rather, the program is intended to move its participants *toward* achievement of the objective.

In such instances, where judging the program completely on the basis of outcomes may be impractical or inappropriate, program evaluation can focus primarily on *implementation.* Program staff can at least be held accountable for providing materials and sponsoring activities that should help people progress toward future goals. Alternative school programs, retraining programs within a company, programs responding to desegregation mandates, and other programs involving shifts of personnel or students are examples of cases where evaluation may well focus principally on implementation. Though these programs may result in remote or fuzzy learning outcomes, the nature of their proper implementation can often be precisely specified.

(2) Creating a lasting description of the program. The summative evaluator's written report may be the only description of the program remaining after it ends. This report should therefore provide an accurate account of the program and include sufficient detail so that it can serve as a basis for planning by those who decide to reinstate the program at another site or in revised form. Such future audiences of your report need to know the characteristics of the site and the sorts of activities and

materials that most likely brought about the program's outcomes.

(3) Providing a list of the possible causes of a program's effects. While such cases are unusual, a summative evaluation that uses a highly controlled design and valid outcome measures can constitute a research study. It can serve as a test of the hypothesis that the particular program activities and materials produce good achievement and attitudes. Here the summative report about a particular program has something to say to policymakers about programs using similar processes or aiming toward similar goals. The activities and materials described in the evaluator's documentation in this case form the "treatment," the independent or manipulated variables in an educational experiment. For example, if a certain percentage of overweight children are randomly assigned to a special health class to study the dangers of obesity, the class constitutes an experimental treatment, and analyses can compare the effects of this treatment with the nonparticipating control group.

The development of evaluation thinking over the past twenty years has led away from the notion that the quantitative research study is the only or even the ideal form for an evaluation. In cases where variables cannot be easily controlled or where creating a control group will deprive individuals of needed services or training, evaluators should neither lament their fate nor belittle the project. But in those cases where an evaluator has the opportunity to design and conduct a research study in the traditional sense, the opportunity should not be wasted.

Knowing the uses to which your documentation will be put helps you determine how much effort to invest in it. Implementation information collected for the purpose of accountability should focus on producing the required "signals" by examining those activities, administrative changes, or materials that are either specifically required by the program funders or have been put forward by the program's planners as the major means of producing its beneficial effects.

The amount of detail with which you describe these characteristics will depend, in turn, on how precisely planners or funders have specified what should take place. If planners, for example, have prescribed only that a program should use the XYZ Reading Series, measuring implementation will require examining the extent of use of this series. If, on the other hand, they plan to use certain portions of the series with children having, say, problems with reading comprehension, then describing implementation will require that you look at which portions are being used and with whom. You will probably need to look in classrooms to ensure that the proper students· are using XYZ. The program might further specify that teachers working in XYZ with problem readers carry out a daily 10-minute drill, rhythmically reading aloud in a group a paragraph from the XYZ story for the week. If the program has been planned this specifically, then your program description will need to attend to these details as well. As a matter of fact, attention to specific behaviors is a good idea when describing any program where you see certain behaviors occurring routinely. Program descriptions at the level of instructor and student or client behavior help readers visualize what people experience, giving them a good chance to think about what features have helped the participants to learn or change.

In many cases, when an evaluation describes implementation for the purpose of creating a lasting program record, the data you collect can be fairly informal, depending on your audience's willingness to believe you. You may talk with staff members, peruse program records, drop in on class sessions, or quote from the program proposal. If accountability is the major reason for your summative evaluation then you must provide data to show whether—and to what extent—the program's most important events actually did occur. The more skeptical your audience, the greater the necessity for providing formal backup data.

If you need to provide a permanent record of program implementation for the purpose of its eventual replication or expansion, try to cover as many of the program characteristics listed in the Appendix as is possible. The level of detail with which you describe each program feature should equal or exceed the specificity of the program plan, at least when describing the features that the staff consider most crucial to producing program effects. If additional practices typical of the program come to your attention during the evaluation, you should include these. You will need to use sufficient backup data so that neither you nor your audience doubt the accuracy or generality of your description.

In cases where the reason for measuring implementation involves research or where there is potential for controversy about your data and conclusions, you will need to back up your description of the program through systematic measurement, such as coded observations by trained raters, examination of program records, structured interviews or questionnaires, or through the more qualitative approaches described in *How to Use Qualitative Methods in Evaluation* (Volume 4 of the *Program Evaluation Kit*). Carefully planned and executed measurement will enable you to be reasonably certain that the information you report truly describes the situation at hand. In cases where the evaluator him- or herself wants to verify the accuracy of the program description, it is important that the evaluator employs relatively formal measures. Careful measurement is essential if it seems that the program description will have to be defended—that is, if the evaluator may confront a skeptic. An example from a common situation illustrates this.

Example. Charles Wong, working for the Evaluation Office of the State Department of Education, was assigned to evaluate statewide facilities in special education for trainable mentally retarded (TMR) students. Dr. Wong sent a lengthy questionnaire early in the school year to 237 sites, requesting that the chief administrator describe physical facilities; staff qualifications; student characteristics; and the educational, vocational, and recreational programs available. Based on the questionnaire results, Dr. Wong prepared a summary report, parts of which appeared in newspapers statewide.

The State Association for Retarded Children, however, took issue with the evaluation's findings. It claimed that the programs did not by and large operate according to the clear objectives described in the report, and facilities were not as well equipped as the report implied. In response to these serious charges, the State Department of Education directed Dr. Wong to follow up his questionnaire with interviews and observations from a random sample of TMR sites.

What he found—mainly on the basis of observations made by trained raters using checklists he had developed—was that facilities were indeed as well equipped as their administrators had originally said and that the curriculum was organized around worthwhile goals. Day-to-day *classroom practice,* however, made poor use of available equipment and was only roughly keyed to the highly specific and well-stated objectives that most of the sites had copied from the state's TMR program guidelines. Dr. Wong could discover what was actually going on only by taking eyes and ears to the program sites themselves.

Assessing implementation for program improvement

As mentioned previously, the task of the formative evaluator is typically more varied than that of the summative evaluator. Formative evaluation involves not only the critical activities of monitoring implementation and examining and reporting progress; it can also mean assuming a role in the program's planning, development, and refinement. The formative evaluator's responsibilities specifically related to program implementa-

tion usually include ensuring that the program description is accurate
and helping the staff and planners to adjust the program, as discussed
below.

*(1) Ensuring throughout program development, that the program's
official description is kept up-to-date, reflecting how the program is
actually being conducted.* While for small-scale programs this description can be unwritten and agreed upon by the few active staff members,
most programs should be described in a written outline that is
periodically updated. An outline of program processes written before
implementation is usually called a *program plan.* Recording what has
taken place during the program's implementation produces one or more
formative implementation reports. The task of providing such reports—
and often of ensuring the existence of a coherent program plan as
well—falls to the formative evaluator.

In many situations, the formative evaluator's first task is to clarify the
program plan. After all, if the goal is to help the staff improve the
program as it develops, the evaluator and staff need to have a clear idea
at the outset of how it is supposed to look. If you work as a formative
evaluator, do not be surprised to find that the staff have only a vague
planning document. Unless the program relies heavily on commercially
published materials with accompanying procedural guides or the
planners are experienced program developers, planners may take a
wait-and-see attitude about many of the program's critical features. This
attitude need not be bothersome; as long as it does not mask hidden
disagreements among staff members about how to proceed or cover up
uncertainty about the program's objectives, a tentative attitude toward
the program can be healthy. It allows the program to take on the form
that will work best.

The wait-and-see approach gives you, however, the job of recording
what does happen so that when and if summative evaluation takes place,
it will focus on a realistic depiction of the program. An accurate
portrayal of the program will also be useful to those who may plan to
adopt, adapt, or expand the program in the future. The role of the
evaluator as program historian or recorder is an essential one, as it is
often the case that staff people simply have no time for such luxuries.
Even as basic a record as meeting notes, arranged chronologically, can
provide helpful information at a later date.

The topics discussed in the formative report can coincide with the
question groupings outlined in the Appendix. *The amount of detail with
which you describe each aspect of the program should match the level of
detail of the program plan as it evolves.*

(2) Helping the staff and planners to change and add to the program as it develops. In many instances the formative evaluator will become involved in program planning, or at least in designing changes in the program as it assumes a clearer form. How involved he or she becomes will depend on the situation. If a program has been planned in considerable detail and if planners are experienced and well versed in the program's subject matter, then they may want the formative evaluator simply to provide information about whether and how the program is being modified from the program plan.

On the other hand, if planners are inexperienced or if the program was not planned in great detail in the first place, then the evaluator may function like an investigative reporter. The evaluator's first job might be to find out what is happening—to see what is going well and badly in the program. He or she will need to examine the program's activities independent of guidance from the plan, and then help eliminate weaknesses and expand on the program's good features. If this case fits your situation, you may want to use the list of implementation questions in the Appendix as suggestions about what to look for, or you may decide to adopt the naturalistic approach described in *How to Use Qualitative Methods in Evaluation* (Volume 4 of the *Program Evaluation Kit*).

The formative evaluator's service to a staff that wants to improve their program can result in diverse activities. Two such activities are particularly important:

(a) The formative evaluator can provide information that prompts the staff and planners to reflect periodically on whether the program is the one they want. This is necessary because programs installed at a particular site rarely look as they did on paper—or as they did in operation elsewhere. At the same time, you may persuade staff and planners to reexamine their initial thinking about why the activities they have chosen to implement should accomplish the program's goals. Careful examination of a program's rationale, handled with sensitivity to the program's setting, can be an important service of the formative evaluator. The planners should have in mind a sensible notion of cause and effect that relates the desired outcomes to the program as envisioned. Insofar as the program as implemented and the outcomes observed fail to match expectations, the program's rationale may need revision.

(b) Controversies over alternative ways to implement the program may lead the formative evaluator to conduct small-scale pilot studies, attitude surveys, or experiments with newly developed program materials and activities. Program planners, after all, must constantly make decisions about how the program will look. These decisions are usually based on hunches about what will work best or what can be changed most readily. Consider questions such as these: Should all math instruction take place in one session, or should there be two sessions during the day? How much additional paperwork will busy supervisors tolerate? How much follow-up activity can be included in the management training course without detracting from employees' short-term, on-the-job productivity?

These are reasonable questions that can be answered by means of quick opinion surveys or short experiments, using the methods described in most research design texts and in the *Evaluator's Handbook* (Volume 1 of the *Program Evaluation Kit*).[2] A short experiment will require that you select experimental and control groups, and then choose treatments that represent the decision alternatives in question. Such short studies should last long enough to allow the alternatives to show effects. The advantage of performing short experiments will quickly become apparent to you; they provide credible evidence about the effectiveness of alternative program components or practices. At the same time, it must be remembered that the practical environment surrounding most evaluations makes even simple experiments difficult to conduct.

When assessing implementation for program improvement, the form of evaluation reports can and should vary greatly. Informal conversations with an influential staff member may have far greater effect than a typewritten report, particularly a report loaded with statistical tables. Periodic meetings to discuss program concerns and issues may update administrators and staff, forcing them to think about program activities far better than even a short written document can. One well-known evaluator has gone so far as to have program personnel place bets on the likely outcome of data analysis so they will have a vested interest in the results.

In summary, the first question to consider as you begin planning an implementation evaluation asks you to determine the purpose of your study. If you are to document the workings of an established program, you will perform a summative evaluation; if you are instead working with staff to develop or improve a program, you will perform a formative evaluation. Whether you work as a summative or a formative evaluator, you will also need to decide early on how much of your implementation report can rely on anecdotal or conversational information and still be credible, and how much your report needs to be backed up by data produced by formal or systematic data collection. This leads to the second question you must consider when you begin thinking about your implementation evaluation.

Question 2. What Overall Evaluation
Orientation Is Most Appropriate?

While the first question asks you to think about the overall purpose of your evaluation, the second asks you to think, in a general sense, about the orientation, approach, or methodology you will use to collect data. Evaluation literature in recent years has been charged by debate over the value of methods that are variously called responsive, qualitative, naturalistic, ethnographic, or "new paradigm." While each of these terms has its own formal definition, in common usage they together describe evaluation techniques borrowed largely from anthropology and sociology that generate words, rather than numbers, as products. The skills they demand of an evaluator differ from those required in the more traditional approach, but an in-depth description of qualitative evaluation methods is beyond the scope of this book.[3] However, it is important that you decide, before you begin to organize the details of your evaluation plan, whether you will use an approach that is largely quantitative, largely qualitative, or some combination of the two.[4]

The traditional approach to program evaluation is quantitative, borrowing its procedures from the scientific method of the physical and biological sciences. A hypothesis is framed, then data are collected to either support or refute the initial claim. According to this view, through repeated studies science comes ever closer to the truth, describing with increasing accuracy an objective reality that exists apart from any individuals. Until recently, most evaluations employed this approach, an approach validated through its appeal to rationality and its obvious success in advancing humanity's knowledge. In a quantitative approach to evaluation, you find out all that you can about a program by first reading its materials and talking with its personnel, then developing a set of questions you will answer and collecting the information you need to answer these questions. In other words, you decide in advance what the evaluation will do, then conduct a study to do just that. Given the dominance of this approach in the field, it is unlikely that you would ever need to justify your choice of quantitative methods for an evaluation.

Example. Each fall the Parent-Teacher Organization at Boynton Middle School sponsors a school fair. The primary motivation for the yearly event is to raise money, and the only data available from previous years are numerical—how much was spent and how much was taken in. But, in addition to its moneymaking potential, school staff also see the fair as an opportunity to instruct students in various principles of economics and to help them feel self-confident about their ability to raise money for desired purchases. To see if this is educational outcome is actually occurring, Ms. Rose, the building principal, develops a short questionnaire for students that includes questions on specific business content and on their feelings about participating in fair planning and implementation. She writes the questions prior to the fair, based on her knowledge of what usually happens, and has teachers administer the questionnaires on the Monday following the fair. She then summarizes the results and presents them at the next PTA meeting.

In contrast to this approach is the qualitative approach. It is possible for an evaluator with a qualitative mind-set to observe a program in operation with relatively few preconceptions about what to look for. The rationale is simple: If you believe that reality does not exist apart from someone's perception of it, an evaluator at best describes the details he or she observes, allowing the language and events selected by participants to tell their own story. Confidence in the description is increased by collecting and confirming information from a variety of sources. Someone may choose this strategy for a number of reasons:

— Many evaluators consider it the best way to describe a program. Unhampered by preconceptions and prescriptions, qualitative inquirers may set their sights on catching the true flavor of a program, discovering the unique set of elements that make it work and conveying them to the evaluation's audience.
— A qualitative approach may be necessary if there is no written plan for the program you are evaluating and you find that the planner cannot retrospectively construct one with a reasonable degree of consistency. Even if there is a plan, it may be vague or, from your perspective, unrealistic to implement.
— You may discover that the program has varied so much from site to site that common features are not apparent at first.

In any of these cases, you have the option of approaching the evaluation as an anthropologist would approach an unknown culture—by just observing. Implicit in a decision to use qualitative methods are at least two other decisions. First, you will rely heavily on data collection methods that get close to the program, usually interviews and on-site observations or participant-observations. Second, qualitative evaluators typically concentrate on relating what they find, rather than comparing what was to what should have been. This may leave you up in the air at first about how to proceed.

Example. Fearing that individuals were somehow slipping through the cracks in its service network, the Social Welfare Department of a small city decided to centralize its services for runaway youth in a single place. At this facility, experienced counselors would diagnose needs, refer individuals to appropriate agencies, then periodically follow up to ensure that clients did, in fact, receive the services they needed. The head of the agency knew that simple body counts of client intakes would not provide sufficient data on how well the new facility was serving the needs of the community's runaways. She therefore scheduled periodic counselor and client interviews and stopped by the facility regularly. She wrote vignettes describing what she observed, reflecting the attitudes and responses of both runaways and staff, and detailing what happened to clients at the various agencies to which they were referred. Her eventual report demonstrated to the City Council how the new facility had directly and dramatically affected the lives of the individual youths served.

This approach may sound familiar to you. The evaluator's vignettes correspond to how most people share information, and, indeed, a qualitative evaluation in a context free of controversy or skepticism looks very much like what people intuitively do when they want to evaluate a program. The difference between such an evaluation, however, and a formal qualitative evaluation is in the quality of the observations made. Qualitative evaluators use methods from the social sciences to obtain corroboration for their observations and conclusions. They have, in fact, developed a method for conducting evaluations that follows that of naturalistic field studies. An evaluation using qualitative methods typically follows a scenario something like this:

(1) A particular program is to be evaluated. If there are numerous sites, one or more sites are chosen for study.
(2) The evaluator gains entry at the site or sites chosen, taking care to establish rapport with program personnel and not to offend anyone. He or she observes activities at the program sites, perhaps even taking part, but trying to influence program routine as little as possible. Issues and concerns of program staff generate questions the evaluation attempts to answer. Often time constraints require the use of informants—people who have already observed events and who are willing to be interviewed at length.

(3) Though data collection can take the form of coded records (such as those produced through the standard observation methods described in Chapter 6), the naturalistic observer more often records what he or she sees in the form of field notes. This choice of recording method is motivated mainly by a desire to avoid deciding too soon which aspects of the situation observed will be considered most important.

(4) The qualitative observer shifts back and forth between formal data collection, informal conversations with the subjects, and analysis of recorded notes. This portion of the evaluation is not so much a linear process as it is holistic; data collection and analysis occur interactively as an observation or other data suggest categories for the analysis and analyses suggest additional data needs. Gradually the evaluator produces a description of the events and an interpretation of them. The report is usually an oral or written narrative, although naturalistic studies can yield tables, sociograms, and other numerical and graphic summaries as well.

The distinction this chapter makes between quantitative and qualitative approaches is helpful in that it separates evaluations that determine in advance what their focus is from those that allow the setting and initial observations to determine what will be observed and how. Despite this conceptual clarity, however, confusion sometimes arises about the methodological orientation of an implementation evaluation. Some people incorrectly assume that any study using interviews is *necessarily* qualitative and that any study that includes questionnaires is *necessarily* quantitative. This is not the case. Either approach can use a variety of methods, including interviews, questionnaires, and observations. Where the approaches differ is in their philosophical bases and, typically, in their final products.

Other people mistakenly assume that if they conduct an informal program evaluation that does not generate statistical tables, they are automatically engaged in qualitative research. Again, this simplistic assumption is not true. As quantitative methodologists require extensive training, so too do qualitative evaluators. The proper conduct of a qualitative evaluation may *look* easy, but it is informal only in the sense that evaluators do not develop specific plans and instruments prior to spending time on site. It is simply not the case that qualitative evaluators proceed informally or willy-nilly. Instead they follow a flexible and changing plan that relies on data to determine its next course of action. Anyone who has worked on a qualitative evaluation will agree that the approach is neither casual nor easy.

The little boy who shouted that the emperor was stark naked first suggested the power of the unbiased observer. In evaluation, unbiased observation can bring to light programmatic concerns or strengths that those involved in the ongoing implementation of a program may not have noticed. While quantitative methods enable an evaluator to provide specific information to program personnel on predetermined questions, in a qualitative approach, observations can help create an accurate description of program characteristics as they develop over time. In choosing an overall orientation for your implementation evaluation, you should consider the appropriateness of the quantitative or qualitative approach for providing the information you will need in order to present decision makers with information they will find useful. You should also consider your timeline and available resources, both human and material.

Summary

This introductory chapter has presented an overall rationale for conducting implementation evaluations. It has also asked you to answer two questions as you begin planning your evaluation. The first question concerns the purpose of your evaluation, whether summative or formative. The second question asks you to decide in a general sense whether your methodological orientation will be quantitative, qualitative, or a combination of both. With these questions answered, you are ready to proceed to the more detailed planning steps presented in Chapter 2.

Notes

1. In general, *describing program implementation* is considered synonymous with *measuring attainment of process objectives* or *determining achievement of means-goals,* phrases used by other authors. We prefer, however, not to discuss implementation solely in connection with process goals and objectives. This is because the primary reason for measuring implementation in many evaluations is to describe the program that is occurring—whether or not this matches what was planned. Other times, of course, measurement will be directed solely by prespecified process goals. *Describing program implementation* is broad enough to cover both situations.

2. See, for example, the "Step-by-Step Guide for Conducting a Small Experiment" in the *Evaluator's Handbook* and the Kit book *How to Design a Program Evaluation* (Volumes 1 and 3, respectively).

3. For a more detailed discussion of qualitative methods see *How to Use Qualitative Methods in Evaluation* by Michael Quinn Patton (1987; Volume 4 of the *Program Evaluation Kit*) and other references listed at the end of this book.

4. Some theorists (e.g., Guba & Lincoln, 1981) argue that because the qualitative and quantitative approaches differ so radically in their philosophical bases, it is impossible to conduct an evaluation that simultaneously uses both approaches. While this is theoretically true, in practice evaluators often structure studies that use a quantitative framework to answer certain questions and a qualitative framework to answer others.

For Further Reading

Fetterman, D. M., & Pitman, M. A. (Eds.). (1985). *Beyond the status quo: Theory, politics and practice in ethnographic evaluation.* Washington, DC: Cato Institute.

Fitz-Gibbon, C. T., & Morris, L. L. (1987). *How to design a program evaluation.* Newbury Park, CA: Sage.

Guba, E. G., & Lincoln, Y. S. (1981). *Effective evaluation.* San Francisco: Jossey-Bass.

Herman, J. L., Morris, L. L., & Fitz-Gibbon, C. T. (1987). *Evaluator's handbook.* Newbury Park, CA: Sage.

Patton, M. Q. (1986). *Utilization-focused evaluation* (2nd ed.). Newbury Park, CA: Sage.

Patton, M. Q. (1987). *How to use qualitative methods in evaluation.* Newbury Park, CA: Sage.

Scriven, M. (1967). The methodology of evaluation. In R. W. Tyler et al. (Eds.), *Perspectives of curriculum evaluation* (pp. 39-83; AERA Monograph Series on Curriculum Evaluation 1). Chicago: Rand McNally.

Chapter 2
Initial Planning:
Deciding What to Measure

Once you determine the purposes that your implementation study will serve and have an overall sense of the methodology you will use, you need to identify the specific questions your evaluation will address and the level of detail with which you will describe the program. Before planning data collection on program implementation, you will first need to answer two additional questions:

(1) *Decide what to look for: Which features of the program are most critical or valuable to describe?* This may amount to deciding which of the questions in the Appendix you will use. Your answer will depend, in part, on how much time and money you have. It will also be affected by your relation to the staff and the funding agency, the announced major components of the program, and the amount of variation suggested by its planners.

(2) *Decide how much effort will be required: What data are needed to support the accuracy of the description of each program characteristic?* Decisions about backup evidence will determine whether your report simply announces the existence of a program feature or offers evidence to support the description you have written. This decision will also be constrained by time and money, as well as by your own judgments about the need for corroboration and the amount of variation you have found in the program. You may want to refer to *How to Focus an Evaluation* (Volume 2 of the *Program Evaluation Kit*).

If you feel that your experience with evaluation or with the program, staff, or funding agency is sufficient to allow you to make these decisions right now, then turn to Chapter 3 and begin planning your data collection. If you do not yet feel ready to do this, the two questions discussed in this chapter will help you decide what to look at and how to substantiate your report.

Question 1. What Are the Program's
Critical Characteristics?

Three categories of features common to all programs can form an initial outline of a program's critical characteristics: its context; its activities; and its theory of action. You can begin to describe the program by outlining the elements of the program's *context*—the tangible features of the program and its setting:

— the classrooms, schools, districts, offices, or sites where the program exists
— the program staff, including administrators, instructors, aides, volunteers, secretaries, and others
— the resources used, including materials constructed or purchased and equipment, particularly resources purchased especially for the program
— the students or participants, including their number, the particular characteristics that made them eligible, and their level of competence at the beginning of the program

The context features constitute the bare bones of the program and must be included in any summary report. Listing them does not require much data-gathering on your part since they are not the sort of data that you expect anyone to challenge or view with skepticism. Unless you have doubts about the delivery of materials or you think that the wrong people are participating, there is little need for backup data to support your description.

Another part of the context you should consider is intangible but may include essential features for understanding program functioning. This is the political context in which the program operates. It includes, for example, understanding what interest groups or powerful individuals are involved in the program, how funding was initially secured, the role of top managers, problems encountered in the program, and so forth. In some settings, none of this will matter; in others, such information will allow you to target your evaluation on areas where you can realistically expect change. While such information is unlikely to appear in formal evaluation documents, only a naive evaluator works without an awareness of the political context—and does so at his or her own risk and at the risk of the evaluation.

After context features, *program activities* are the second topic to describe as critical characteristics. Describing important activities demands formulating and answering questions about *how* the program was implemented, for example:

— What materials were used? Were they used as indicated?

— What procedures were prescribed for program staff in their interactions with clients? Were these procedures followed?
— In what activities were program participants supposed to participate? Did they?
— What activities were prescribed for other participants (e.g., management, assistants, volunteers, tutors)? Did they engage in them?
— What administrative arrangements did the program include? What lines of authority were to be used for making important decisions? What changes occurred in these arrangements?

Listing salient intended program activities will, of course, take you much less time than verifying that they *have* occurred and in what form. Unlike materials that usually stay put and whose presence can be checked at practically any time, program activities may be inaccessible once they have occurred if they were not consciously observed or recorded. Counting them or merely noting their presence is therefore no small task. In addition, activities are more difficult to recognize than context features. Lectures, microcomputers, aides, and instructional materials from Company Z are easily identified; but what exactly does *reinforcement* or *acceptance of a student's cultural background* look like in practice? You simply cannot observe and report instances of activities such as reinforcement and cultural acceptance as you can an inventory of materials or a head count of participants. And even if specific instances can be directly observed, you cannot possibly describe all of them. *You will therefore have to choose which activities to attend to.* Your choice of these activities will in large measure depend on what your audience needs to know in order to make informed decisions.

Once you delineate context and activities, you may begin to infer a third and often difficult program feature to determine—what can be called the program's *theory of action.* Every program, no matter how small, operates with some theoretical notion of cause and effect. Theories underlying programs may be implicit or explicit, intuitive or formal, specific or general. Some programs evolve their own informal theories, combining common sense, practice, and theoretical tenets from a variety of sources. Examples surround us: If teenage parents learn parenting skills, their children will eat more nutritiously; if bilingual students receive reinforcement in their native language, their cognitive skills will develop normally; if long-term employees participate in certain management decisions, their job productivity will increase. Or consider this more detailed example.

Example. Mr. Appelbaum, the director and de facto formative evaluator of in-service training programs at a large city school staff development center, noticed that some schools allowed teachers free choice of activities. Others, believing that in-service trainihg should follow a theme, encouraged teachers to select activities within a single area—say elementary math or higher-order thinking skills.

Though the staff development center itself made no recommendations about what activities should be pursued, Mr. Appelbaum decided that the "theme versus no-theme" flavor of teacher training might have an effect on teachers' overall assessment of the value of their in-service experiences. He decided to describe the course of study of the two groups of teachers at the center and separately analyze the groups' responses to an attitude questionnaire.

As Mr. Appelbaum expected, teachers whose training followed a theme expressed greater enthusiasm about the staff development center. Since he could find no explanation for the difference in enthusiasm between the two groups other than the thematic character of one group's program, Mr. Appelbaum recommended that the center itself encourage thematic in-service study. He used his descriptions of the courses of study of the teachers in the theme group as a set of models the center might follow.

Mr. Appelbaum, in the example above, worked from the rather rudimentary but verifiable theory that education organized as a program of study is more likely to be perceived by the student as valuable. His evaluation was at least partly theory-based because he used an implicit theory to tell him what to look at.

Other programs are systematically designed to implement the tenets of a model or theory of behavior (e.g., teaching, learning, organizational behavior) or of a philosophy concerning children, social programs, or organizations. A theory-based implementation evaluation is especially appropriate for looking at such programs. The specific prescriptions of many such models and theories are familiar to most people working in education or the social services.[1] Examples of some of these models include the following:

— behavior modification and various applications of reinforcement theory to instruction, classroom discipline, substance abuse, juvenile and adult offenders
— Piaget's theory of cognitive development and other models of how children learn concepts
— fifth-year teacher education programs that require students to become completely well versed in a scholarly discipline prior to pedagogical studies

— fundamental school, competency-based, and basic skills models that seek to reinstate traditional American classroom practices
— physical, affective, and behavioral models underlying health and fitness programs
— models of organization (e.g., quality circles) that prescribe arrangements and procedures for effective management
— group process models which underlie social action and other intervention programs
— counseling models underlying approaches to child abuse prevention

To the extent that you base what to look for on a set of assumptions about what works in an instructional or social program, you are conducting what can be called a "theory-based" evaluation. The job for the evaluator is to discover the theory of action in order to better understand how the program is supposed to work and what its critical characteristics are in the eyes of program planners and staff. A program identified with any of these points of view must set up roles and procedures consistent with the particular theory or value system.

Proponents of open schools, for example, would agree that a classroom reflecting their point of view should display freedom of movement, individualization of instruction, and curricular choices made by students. Each theory, philosophy, or teaching model contends that *particular activities* either are worthwhile in and of themselves or are the best way to promote certain desirable outcomes. Assessing implementation of a theory-based program, then, becomes a matter of checking the extent to which activities or organizational arrangements at the program sites reflect the theory. Theory-based evaluation may also involve your assessment of the consistency of the program plan with the underlying theory.

In summative evaluations based on a credible research design, a theory-based evaluation can provide an actual *test* of the theory's validity. Given the potential importance and rarity of empirical validation of a theory, you should disseminate results of an evaluation that provides such validation as widely as possible.

Example. Mr. MacCallum heads an in-service instructional unit within a large company whose products have changed dramatically with the advance of computer theory and technology. Managers are concerned that a lack of expertise in theoretical computer science hinders the performance of engineers hired before 1970. Most of these individuals are highly skilled at their work, but solve technical problems with cumbersome, seat-of-the-pants solutions rather than the efficient and elegant solutions a more theoretical approach would suggest. With the help of a university professor who conducts research on the effects of structured programming, Mr. MacCallum establishes a series of two-week courses to teach basic computer science concepts to engineers who have not taken a technical course since their graduation from college. The theory in action behind MacCallum's program is the following: Career engineers who understand the principles of structured programming will apply them to on-the-job technical problems more efficiently; this will make them more confident of their skill, less threatened by new hires, and should ultimately lead both to higher levels of productivity and to improved products. Evaluators of this in-service program face a difficult job in trying to demonstrate its long-term effects, but company management supports the program because of the potential benefits implicit in its theory of action.

On paper it may sound relatively straightforward to describe a program's context, key activities, and theory of action, but in practice critical details may prove elusive. Your search for these critical program features should rely on three sources of information: (1) the program proposal or plan; (2) people's opinions, based on assumptions about what makes an instructional or social program work; and (3) your own observations.

Picking out critical characteristics
from the program proposal

Some proposals will come right out and list the program's most important features, perhaps even explaining *why* planners think these materials and activities will bring about the desired outcomes. Many will include such a list, although if you look carefully you may find clues about what is considered important. For instance, most proposals or documents describing a program will refer repeatedly to certain *key activities.* As a rule of thumb, the more frequently an activity is cited, the more critical someone considers it to be for program success. You may therefore decide that activities *repeatedly mentioned* are critical program components to which the evaluation must attend.

The program's *budget* is another index to its critical features. As another rule of thumb, you may assume that the larger the budgeted dollar or other resource expenditure (such as staff level) for a particular program feature—activity, event, material, or configuration of program elements—the greater its contribution is presumed to be to program success. Taken together, these two planning elements—frequency of citation and level of expenditure or effort—provide some indication of the program's critical components.

Relying on the program plan for suggestions about *what* to describe determines a point of view from which to approach your implementation evaluation. An implementation evaluation based largely on the program plan will involve collecting data to determine the extent to which the crucial activities described in the plan occurred as intended—and if they did not occur as planned, what happened instead. Program descriptions of this type are common, and for an understandable reason: They provide the simplest means by which the evaluator can decide what activities to look at.

Example. A university-based health educator wrote a proposal to a local foundation to implement a smoking cessation program for staff at Crescent City University. The program was to be based largely on purchased audio-visual materials. The evaluator who examined the program relied heavily on the original proposal as a program description. To complete the documentation section of his summative report, he simply noted the program's official description and observed informally to locate consistencies and discrepancies between the planned program and the one that actually occurred.

The program plan can be a rich source of details about a program. But because it is a written document produced *prior to* the program's implementation, it can also limit your focus. To rely solely on a program proposal is to assume that what is written is all that is important, and this is often not the case. If you have reason to believe that some feature *not mentioned* in the program's planning documents may be necessary for program success, then look for that feature. Commonly unmentioned but critical program characteristics in educational programs, for instance, include *opportunities for students to practice what they learn, adequate time on task,* and *teacher training.* Planners of instructional programs, it seems, spend a lot of time deciding what to teach and in what sequence, but often overlook students' need to practice the information they have learned and teachers' need to change how they teach.

You should also consider features not specifically cited in the program plan whose presence may be related to program failure. You may incidentally discover a feature of the program that could actually make it fail. By all means pay attention to this kind of information, backing up your description with data. If you are a formative evaluator, it is, in fact, your responsibility to bring such matters to the attention of the staff.

A related problem with relying on the program plan as a source of critical features comes from its basis in what has been called the rational goal attainment model. To look only at how closely a program comes to attaining its stated objectives is to put blinders on the evaluation. Perhaps the goals themselves are inappropriate, so that whether or not they are attained is beside the point. Or perhaps the program attains its goals, but at the same time creates potentially negative side effects. Any evaluator using the program plan to locate critical features should be aware of the limitations of this approach.

Considering people's opinions to determine critical program features

In some instances you may find the program plan to be a disappointing source of ideas about what to look for. It may not describe proposed activities to the degree of specificity you feel you need; or it may express grandiose plans, engendered by initial enthusiasm or by responding to funding guidelines that were themselves overly ambitious. It is possible, as well, that the program *has not been planned* in any specific way. How, then, will you document the program if there is no plan detailing activities that are specific, feasible, and consistent?

In this case, you have three options. First, in the absence of a formal written program plan, you can document implicit planning by interviewing program planners and asking them to describe activities they feel are crucial to the program. (In fact, even in the presence of a written plan, you would want to verify your understandings of critical program features by interviewing program planners.) You can then proceed to document the occurrence of these activities. Second, in theory-based programs you can consult experts in the field to determine the features that they think *should* appear in a properly designed program. Finally, you can rely on your own intuition and experience to propose the features that you would expect to find in the program.

Using observation to determine critical program features

The evaluator who chooses qualitative methods will read program documents and talk with staff, but will gain a great deal of information through direct observation of program activities. Over time the critical features of the program as implemented will emerge from analyses of field notes.

Regardless of how you determine the list of critical characteristics, a listing of the critical features of the program will give you some notion of which questions in the Appendix your implementation evaluation will answer. If you are a summative evaluator, then your task will be to convey to your audience as complete a depiction of the program's crucial characteristics as possible.

If you are a formative evaluator, then your decision about what to look at may have to go a step beyond listing the program's critical features. Since your job is to help with program improvement and not merely to describe the program, your task is to collect information that will be maximally useful *in helping program staff to improve the program.* In most cases, this will certainly mean monitoring the implementation of the program's most critical features. But you will need to consult with the program staff to find which among all the program's critical features seem most troublesome to them, most in need of vigilant attention, or most amenable to change. It could be, for instance, that a program's most critical feature is employment of aides. But once the aides have arrived and it has been established that they come to work regularly, attention to this detail may no longer be necessary. Your formative service to the program will be more usefully employed in monitoring the implementation of program aspects about which the staff have genuine problems to solve.

Planned variation

Your choice of which program characteristics to describe will be influenced by the *amount of variation* that occurs across sites where the program is being used and by the amount of variation across time. In general, greater variation means there is more to pay attention to. Some programs, after all, encourage variation. Directors of such programs have said to the staff or delegates at different sites something like the following:

> The central curriculum office has chosen a reading program that we can purchase with our new federal compensatory education money. Take the program and use it as you think best suits your students and teachers. Adapt the program features to meet your needs.

It is likely that an evaluator—either formative[2] or summative—will be called in to examine the entire federal compensatory education program, and the evaluator will most likely find many versions of the program taking place. Such implementation has been called "mutual adaptation" since program personnel are expected to adapt the stated plans to their given context. In such cases, the evaluator must describe implementation of each program interpretation separately. Planned variation, incidentally, provides a good opportunity to collect information that may prove useful to future planning in this district or elsewhere. The evaluator can compare the ease and success of program implementation across sites. Where different programs have resulted at sites that are otherwise similar, the evaluator can compare results to gain clues about the relative effectiveness of the program implementation.

Program directors could have encouraged even more program variation by saying, "We have X dollars to improve our reading program for the educationally disadvantaged. Take these funds and put together a new program." This kind of directive produces programs whose only common features across sites are likely to be the target students and the funding source. While variation is also *planned* in this situation, unlike the program in the preceding example each site has been left free to create its own unique program. The districtwide evaluator may have to look at each version of the program that emerges, probably adopting either theory-based or qualitative methods. Though the evaluator may find a chance to make comparisons among the program versions put into effect at different sites, he or she will probably spend a great deal of time *discovering* and reporting what each program variation looks like. However, the simple act of telling the implementers about the various forms the program has taken will be useful. Most probably some forms of the program will be more easily implemented, produce better results, or be more popular than others.

If the evaluator—whether summative or formative—should uncover variation across sites or over time that has *not* been planned, then he or she should describe these findings, collecting backup data if it seems that corroborating evidence will be necessary.

Constructing a list of program characteristics

Composing a list of critical characteristics is the first step in each of the data-gathering procedures outlined in Chapters 4, 5, and 6. Constructing an accurate list early in your evaluation will help ensure that program decision makers receive credible information that will be useful later. This chapter has discussed a variety of sources for critical characteristics. A thoughtful look through the program's plan or proposal, a talk with staff and planners, your own thinking about what the program should look like (perhaps based on its underlying theory or philosophy), and on-site observations should help you arrive at a list of the program materials, activities, processes, or administrative procedures whose implementation you want to track. The list of implementation evaluation questions in the Appendix may help you to establish priorities among your own questions or to double-check that you have not neglected something important.

No matter how you find them out, you should make sure of two things: (1) that the program features you list are those considered crucial to the program by the staff, planners, and other audiences; and (2) that the list is sufficiently detailed. Detailed in this case means that the list should include a prescription of the frequency or duration of activities and of their form (who, what, where, how) that is specific enough to allow you to picture each activity in your head.

The program characteristics list can take any form that is useful to you. If you think you may later use it in a summative report or as a vehicle for reporting to staff, consider using a format such as the one in Table 2. The information in this or similar tables can serve as a standard against which to assess implementation. For summative evaluation, Table 2 can convey the adequacy of implementation by adding two additional columns at the right:

gress	Assessment of adequacy of implementation	supporting data
of SMA, all		
ed		

You may prefer to begin with a less elaborate program characteristics list than is shown in Table 2. The following example presents a simpler one.

Example. In an effort to secure the assistance of young people during peak attendance hours, the Metropolis Zoo established the Youth Educator Training Program. The description of the program included the following paragraph:

Docents experienced in a given area (e.g., the Asian Domain, the Children's Zoo) will be assigned one to three students. Tutoring

TABLE 2

Program Ex-Cell Implementation Description

Program Component:
4th Grade Reading Comprehension--Remedial Activities

Person responsible for implementation	Target group	Activity	Materials	Organization for activity	Frequency/ duration	Amount of progress expected
Teacher	Students	Vocabulary drill and games	SMA word cards, 3rd & 4th level	Small groups (based on CTBA vocabulary score)	Daily, 15-20 minutes	Completion of SMA, Level 4, by all students
			Teacher-developed word cards, vocabulary	Same	Same	None specified
			Old Maid	Same	Same	None specified
Teacher/Aide	Students	Language experience activities --keeping a diary, writing stories	Student notebooks, primary and elite typewriters	Individual	Productions checked weekly (Fridays); students work at self-selected times or at home	Completion of at least one 20-page notebook by each child; 80% of students judged by teacher or aide as "making progress"
Reading specialist/ teacher, student tutors	Students	Peer tutoring within class, in readers and workbooks	United States Book Company Urban Children reading series and workbooks	Student tutoring dyads	Monday through Thursday, 20-30 minutes	Completion of 1+ grade levels by 80% of students
Principal	Parents	Outreach--inform parents of progress; encourage at-home work in Urban Children texts; hold two Parents' nights; periodic conferences		All parents for program come to Parents' Night; other contact with parents on individual basis	Two Parents' Nights--Nov. and Mar.; 3 written progress reports in Dec., Apr., June; other contact with parents ad hoc	

activities will take place in two-hour sessions over five weekends with a sixth weekend reserved for make-ups. The first three sessions, held at the Education Center, will cover the content contained in the appropriate Metropolis Zoo Guide and related material on permanent exhibit in the center. The final two sessions will be on-the-job training, with the docent demonstrating proper procedures for interacting with the public and providing additional information as needed.

The assistant curator, assigned to monitor the program's implementation, constructed a list of program characteristics from the written plan that included the clarifying questions she would ask in initial meetings:

Youth Educator Training Activities

— Who—experienced docents (selected how?); interested high school students (recruited how?); ratio of 1:3 maximum (why so few?)
— What—content of zoo guide for appropriate domain; material on exhibit in center; interpersonal skills (director says these are being formally written up; are they appropriate for this age?)
— When—frequency: 5 sessions; duration: 2 hours (is this sufficient?)
— Where—sessions 1-3: Education Center; sessions 4-5: on-site
— Why—exactly what are the "youth educators" to do? (are they to function exactly as the docents do, or is there to be something special about their presence?)
— How will we know the program is working? number of participants? their "effectiveness"? other things? (who can decide this?)

Regardless of its form, when your list of critical features if completed, you are ready to consider a second question in your initial planning.

Question 2. How Much Supporting Data Do You Need?

You may need to describe program implementation for people who are at some distance from the program, either in location or familiarity. These people will base their opinions about the program's form and quality on what they read in your description. You may therefore need to provide backup data to verify the accuracy of your description.

If the description you produce is for people *close* to the program and familiar with it, then you can rely on the audience's detailed knowledge of the program in operation—at least in their own setting. In such a case, you may want to focus your data collection on the extent to which the program's implementation at one site is representative of its implementation at other sites. The credibility of your report for people close to the program will, of course, depend on how well your description of the program matches what they perceive. If you feel that your report of overall program implementation diverges considerably from the experiences of the program's administration or of participants at any one site, then you may need to collect good, hard backup data.

These are examples of more specific circumstances calling for backup data:

—summative evaluations that constitute research studies addressed to the profession and to the community at large
—evaluations aimed at providing new information for a situation where there is likely to be controversy
—evaluations calling for program implementation descriptions so detailed that they characterize program activity at the level of individual behaviors
—descriptions of programs that may be used as a basis for adopting or adapting the program in other settings
—descriptions of programs that have varied considerably from site to site or from time to time

How you use backup data will be determined in part by which of the three approaches described earlier you adopt:

(1) Using the program plan as a baseline and examining how well the program as implemented fits the plan.
(2) Using a theory or model to decide the features that should be present in the program. In this case you will probably consult research literature or various experts for guidance in what to look for. In both this and the plan-based approaches, backup data will be necessary to permit people to judge how closely the actual program fits what was planned. Such data can also help you document unplanned program features.
(3) Entering without preconceptions and instead taking a naturalistic stance toward the evaluation. In this situation you will attempt to enter the program sites with no initial preconceptions or assumptions about what the program should look like.

If you assume either of the first two points of view, your final report will describe the fit of the program to the prescription you have chosen. In the third situation, your final report will simply describe the program that you found, noting, of course, variability from site to site.

Summary

This chapter has discussed assessing program implementation with a view toward making this aspect of your evaluation sensitive to the needs of your audiences and the context in which you are working. To help ensure that your reports will be useful and credible, this chapter has discussed the initial planning decisions you should make *before* you begin your evaluation, determining which features of the program your evaluation should focus on and how well you will substantiate your description of the program. Having made these decisions, you are now ready to move on to Chapter 3 to plan exactly how you will collect data for your implementation evaluation.

Notes

1. An excellent presentation of the implications of various models of schooling and education is put forth in Joyce and Weil's (1986) *Models of Teaching*.

2. Where there is *one* formative evaluator working with the program throughout the district, agency, or organization, he or she will become involved with assessing variation and perhaps sharing ideas across sites. Where there is a separate formative evaluator *at each site*, each evaluator will work according to different priorities. The job of each evaluator will be to see that *each* version of the program develops as well as possible, perhaps disregarding what other sites are doing.

For Further Reading

Evertson, C. M., & Green, J. L. (1986). Observation as inquiry and method. In *Handbook of Research on Teaching* (3rd. ed.). New York: MacMillan.

Joyce, B., & Weil, M. (1986). *Models of Teaching* (3rd. ed.) Englewood Cliffs, NJ: Prentice-Hall.

Chapter 3
Planning for Data Collection

Chapter 1 listed reasons for including an accurate program description in your evaluation report. These reasons included the need to document that the program staff delivered the service they promised, to set down a concrete description of the program that can be used for its replication, and to provide a basis for thinking about relationships between implementation and program effects. The summative evaluator will document a program's implementation for one or more of these purposes. The formative evaluator, on the other hand, will primarily be concerned with tracking how the program evolves and how it changes, keeping a record of its developmental history and giving feedback to the program staff about flaws and successes in the process of program installation.

Chapter 2 focused on two questions. At some early point in your thinking about implementation evaluation, you will need to decide which characteristics of the program you will describe and make a related decision about which of these descriptions need substantiating— that is, which parts of your report need to be backed up by data.

In this chapter you will begin planning for data collection. The simplest way to document program activities, materials, and administration—but, unfortunately, the least adequate for most purposes—is to use an existing description of the program (i.e., the plan or proposal) to double as your program implementation report. If you are severely pressed by time or other constraints and if such a plan exists, you may be able to get by with this. But if you or a member of your staff have time to spend actually collecting implementation data, then your description of the program will be richer and subsequently more credible and useful. If you are a formative evaluator whose job is to report what is occurring at program sites, you cannot help but become involved in such data collection. For those who will collect data, this chapter discusses several key concerns for obtaining data for your report. It takes you through five steps in planning for data collection:

(1) choosing data collection methods
(2) determining whether appropriate measures already exist
(3) creating a sampling strategy
(4) thinking about validity and reliability
(5) planning for data analysis

Step 1. Choosing data collection methods

This book introduces you to three common approaches for collecting supporting data for your implementation report: (1) examining records; (2) using self-report measures; and (3) conducting observations. The use of any one method does not exclude the use of others, and there are no simple rules to guide your selection. The method or combination of methods you select will be primarily a function of three factors: the overall purpose of your evaluation; the information needs of your audience; and the practical constraints on the evaluation process.

Method 1. Examine the records kept over the course of the program. The first method of data collection requires that you examine the program's existing records. These might include sign-in sheets for materials, library loan records, individual assignment cards, attendance sheets, instructors' logs of classroom activities, disposition records, intake logs or referral records. In a program where extensive records are kept as a matter of course, you may be able to extract from them a substantial part of the data you need to determine what activities occurred and who did what with whom. This method will yield credible evaluation information because it accumulates evidence of program events as they occurred rather than reconstructing them later. If records are routinely kept as part of the program, their use also makes your data collection rather unobtrusive.

The use of existing records, however, is not without major drawbacks. First, abstracting information from them can be time-consuming. Second are problems of data quality and completeness. Third, records kept over the course of the program will probably not meet all of your data collection requirements. If it looks as though the existing records are inadequate, you have two alternatives. The best one is to set up your own record-keeping system, assuming, of course, that you have arrived on the scene in time to do this. A weaker alternative is to gather recollected versions of program records from participants. Should you do this, point out in your report the extent to which this information is corroborated by more formal records or results from other measures.

Method 2. Use self-report measures. A second data collection

method involves asking key program personnel and key participants—
administrators, teachers, staff, clients, students, or community members—to describe what program activities looked like. It makes sense, of
course, to turn to the people who have experienced a program for
information about it. You may gather such information through
interviews, through questionnaires, or through a combination of both.
Usually, of course, you will not be able to collect information from
everyone who worked in or was affected by the program—it would take
too much effort and time. Instead you will want to sample people within
each important role group. Since different groups of program participants may have divergent perceptions, you may want to gather self-
report information, probably on a sample basis, from all key groups
(e.g., teachers, managers, staff, volunteers, and students/clients) and
then compare the information provided by different groups to see if you
develop a consistent set of pictures about the program.

Be aware that, depending on the situation, self-report measures can
have credibility problems. While people close to the program will find
such information credible, people far from the program—for instance,
at the funding agency or in management—are less likely to trust self-
report information from the staff. They may worry, first of all, that your
respondents have a vested interest in making the program look good.
Second, even when intentional bias is unlikely, self-report descriptions
are at best secondhand accounts of what transpired—the evaluator tells
the audience what people say they did. Third, self-report information
often consists of after-the-fact recollections of people's own actions.
Accounts of what people remember having done themselves often are
not as credible as descriptions by impartial others who actually saw
what was done.

Because of credibility problems and the need for detailed program
implementation description, self-report instruments are more often
used to verify or to check the consistency across sites of a program
description arrived at by more direct means. Only when the evaluator's
resources are too limited to permit collection of close-up observation
data should self-report measures constitute the primary source of
implementation information.

Method 3. Conduct observations. A final data collection method
involves actual observations of program activities, with one or more
observers making periodic visits to program sites to record their
observations, either freely or according to a predetermined list of
categories. Although it can require a great deal of time and effort,
on-site observation is highly credible because an impartial observer

watches or even participates in program events as they occur. Such credibility can be even further enhanced by demonstrating that the data from the observations are reliable, that is, consistent across different observers and over time.

To help you in thinking about which methods of data collection are appropriate for your own situation, Table 3 summarizes the advantages and disadvantages of each of the methods. The next three chapters then present each of the three data collection methods in greater detail.

Chapter 4 discusses how to use records to assess program implementation, describing both how to check program records that already exist and how to set up your own record-keeping system. Chapter 5 describes how to use self-report instruments with staff members, participants, and others, giving step-by-step procedures for constructing and administering questionnaires and for conducting interviews. Chapter 6 discusses program observations, describing methods for conducting formal observations.

In making decisions about data collection, keep in mind that your study will be more valid and credible if data from several sources converge on the same picture. This requires using multiple measures and multiple data collection methods and gathering data from different participants at different sites. For example, if you were evaluating a program aimed at individualization, you might want to document the extent to which instruction really was determined according to individual needs. To ensure that you obtain enough evidence, you could collect different kinds of data. Perhaps you would interview students at the various program sites about the sequence and pacing of their lessons and the extent to which instruction occurs in groups. To corroborate what you found through student interviews, you might examine the teachers' record-keeping systems. In an individualized program it is likely that teachers maintain charts or prescription forms that track individual student progress. Finally, you might conduct a few observations or spot checks, watching typical classes in session to estimate the amount of individual instruction and progress-monitoring per student, both within and across sites. Three sources of information-interviews, examination of records, and observation—could then be reported, each supporting or qualifying the findings of the others.

Step 2. Determining whether appropriate measures already exist

Before you involve yourself in the onerous business of designing your own implementation measures, you may want to consider using instruments already available. Educational researchers have developed

TABLE 3

Method 1: Examine Records.

Records are systematic accounts of regular occurrences consisting of such things as attendance and enrollment reports, sign-in sheets, library checkout records, permission slips, counselor files, teacher logs, individual student assignment cards, etc.

Method 2: Conduct Observations.

Observations require that one or more observers devote all their attention to the behavior of an individual or group within a natural setting and for a prescribed time period. In some cases, an observer may be given detailed guidelines about who or what to observe, when and how long to observe, and the method of recording the information. An instrument to record this kind of information would likely be formatted as a questionnaire or tally sheet. An observer may also be sent into a classroom with less restrictive instructions, i.e., without detailed guidelines, and simply asked to write a responsive/naturalistic account of events which occurred within the prescribed time period.

Method 3: Use Self-Report Measures.

Questionnaires are instruments that present information to a respondent in writing or through the use of pictures and then require a written response—a check, a circle, a word, a sentence, or several sentences.

Interviews involve a face-to-face meeting between two (or more) persons in which a respondent answers questions posed by an interviewer. The questions may be predetermined, but the interviewer is free to pursue interesting responses. The respondent's answers are usually recorded in some way by the interviewer during the interview, but a summary of the responses is generally completed afterwards.

Methods for Collecting Implementation Data

Advantages	Disadvantages
• Records kept for purposes other than the program evaluation can be a source of data gathered without additional demands on people's time and energies. • Records are often viewed as objective and therefore credible. • Records set down events at the time of occurrence rather than in retrospect. This also increases credibility.	• Records may be incomplete. • The process of examining them and extracting relevant information can be time-consuming. • There may be ethical or legal constraints involved in your examination of certain kinds of records —counselor files for example. • Asking people to keep records specifically for the program evaluation may be seen as burdensome.
• Observations can be highly credible when seen as the report of what actually took place presented by disinterested outsider(s). • Observers provide a point of view different from that of people most closely connected with the program.	• The presence of observers may alter what takes place. • Time is needed to develop the observation instrument and train observers if the observation is highly prescribed. • It is necessary to locate credible observers if the observation is not carefully controlled. • Time is needed to conduct sufficient numbers of observations. • There are usually scheduling problems.
• Questionnaires provide the answers to a variety of questions. • They can be answered anonymously. • They allow the respondent time to think before responding. • They can be given to many people, at distant sites, simultaneously. • They can be mailed. • They impose uniformity on the information obtained by asking all respondents the same things, e.g., asking teachers to supply the names of all math games used in class throughout the semester.	• They do not provide the flexibility of interviews. • People are often better able to express themselves orally than in writing. • Persuading people to complete and return questionnaires is sometimes difficult.
• Interviews can be used to obtain information from people who cannot read and from non-native speakers who might have difficulties with the wording of written questions. • Interviews permit flexibility. They allow the interviewer to pursue unanticipated lines of inquiry.	• Interviewing is time-consuming. • Sometimes the interviewer can unduly influence the responses of the interviewee.

some measures, mainly observation schedules and questionnaires, that you can use to describe general characteristics of groups, classrooms, and other educational units. Titles of these instruments often mention school or classroom climate, patterns of interaction and verbal communication, or characteristics of the learning environment. The chief advantage of using such measures is that they have established validity and reliability. But there are disadvantages as well. A key disadvantage is that they may or may not be sensitive to what the program is trying to accomplish or the specific activities and processes that are to be implemented. An excellent instrument that measures the wrong thing still measures the wrong thing and should not, therefore, be used. A second disadvantage associated with these measures is their relative inaccessibility. With the rapid growth of research on classroom interaction, numerous observation instruments and tests have been developed; but it may be difficult to locate them or, in some cases, to afford to use them. Below are listed two anthologies which, although they are rapidly becoming dated, still may be of value to you in your search.

Evaluating Classroom Instruction: A Sourcebook of Instruments (Borich & Madden, 1977) contains a comprehensive review of instruments for evaluating instruction and describing classroom activities. It lists 171 instruments, describes each including its availability, reliability, validity, norms (if any), and procedures for administration and scoring. Each is also briefly reviewed, and sample items are provided. Only measures which have been empirically validated appear in the sourcebook. The instruments are cross-classified according to what the instrument describes (teacher, pupil, or classroom) and who provides the information (the teacher, the pupil, or observer).

Mirrors for Behavior: An Anthology of Classroom Observation Instruments (Simon & Boyer, 1974) provides abstracts of 99 classroom observation systems. Each abstract contains information on the subjects of the observation, the setting, the methods of collecting the data, the type of behavior that is recorded, and the ways in which the data can be used. In addition, an extensive bibliography directs the reader to further information on these and how they have been used by others. An earlier edition of this work (1967) provides detailed descriptions of 26 of these systems.

In addition to the above two anthologies, you may want to refer to three other sources for information on existing instruments: (1) the collection of *Mental Measurement Yearbook,* which contain descriptions and reviews of published tests; (2) a chapter by Evertson and Green (1986) in the *Handbook of Research on Teaching*, which identifies and discusses recent instrument development; and (3) Volume 21, Number 2 of the *Journal of Classroom Interaction*, which contains a summary of topics covered in back issues.

Step 3. Creating a sampling strategy

Unless the program you are examining is small and relatively simple, you will not be able to collect and transcribe data on every student and activity over the course of the entire program. What is more, there is no need to cover the entire spectrum of sites, participants, events, and activities in order to produce a complete and credible evaluation. But you will need to decide early on where the implementation information you do collect will come from. Specifically you must plan

- where to look
- whom to ask or observe
- when to look—and how to sample events and times

Where to look. The first decision concerns how many program sites you should examine. Your answer to this will be determined largely by your choice of measurement method. A questionnaire, for instance, can reach many more places than can an observer. Unless the program is taking place in just a few places, close together, it will probably not be practical or necessary to observe implementation at all of them. A representative sample will provide you with sufficient information to develop an accurate portrayal of the program.

Solving the problem of which sites constitute a representative sample requires that you first group them according to two sets of characteristics:

(1) features of the sites that could affect how the program is implemented— such as size of the population served, geographical location, number of years participation in the program, amount of community or administrative support for the program, level of funding, teacher commitment to the program, student or staff traits or abilities

(2) variations permitted in the program itself that may make it look different at different locations—such as amount of time given to the program per day or week, choice of curricular materials, or omission of some program components such as a management system or audiovisual materials[1]

The list of such characteristics unique to each evaluation may be long. For your own use, choose four or so major sources of program divergence across sites and classify the sites accordingly. Then, based on the number of sites you can realistically examine, randomly choose some to represent each classification. You can, of course, select some sites for intensive study and a pool of others to examine more cursorily.

You also may need, for public relations reasons, to at least make an appearance at every program site. In any case, make certain that you will be allowed access to every site you need to visit. Such access should be established *before* you begin collecting data.

Whom to ask or observe. Regardless of the size of the program or how many sites your implementation evaluation reaches, you will eventually have to talk with, question, or observe people. In most cases, these will be people both within the program—the participants whose behavior it affects—and those outside—parents, administrators, and other contributors to its context. Answers to questions about whether to sample people depend, as with your choice of sites, on the measurement method you will use and on your time and resources.

Whom you approach for information also depends on the willingness of people to cooperate, since implementation evaluation nearly always intrudes on the program or consumes staff time. If you plan to use questionnaires, short interviews, or observations that are either infrequent or of short duration, then you probably can select people randomly. In these cases, applying the clout factor by having a person in authority introduce you and explain your purpose will facilitate cooperation. If you intend to administer questionnaires or interviews for other purposes, perhaps to measure people's attitudes, you may be able to insert a few implementation questions into these. It is often possible and always a good idea to consolidate instruments.

At times your measurement will require a good deal of cooperation. This is the case with requests for record-keeping systems that require continuous maintenance; intensive observation, either formal or naturalistic; and questionnaires and interviews given periodically over time to the same people. If data collection requires considerable effort from the staff, then you will need power, authority, or incentives to back your requests; in the absence of such support, you may want to ask for volunteer participants. Keep in mind, however, that volunteers raise the specter of bias. The advantage of gathering information from people willing to cooperate is that you will be able to report a complete picture of the program; the disadvantage is that you will not know whether everyone shares the same picture, although you can check for possible bias.

Exactly which people should you question or observe? Answers to this will vary, but here are some pointers:

—Ask people, of course, who are likely to know—key staff members and planners. If you think that these people may give you a distorted view, your audience is likely to think so, too. You should back up what official spokespeople tell you by observing or asking others who may be considered more impartial.
—Some of the others should be program participants (students, clients, employees, etc.) if possible. Good information also comes from support staff members such as assistants or secretaries. People in these roles see at least part of the program in operation every day—but they are less likely to know what it is supposed to look like officially.
—Ask people to nominate the individuals who are in the best position to tell you the 'truth' about the program. When the same names are mentioned by several program people, you know that you should carefully consider the information these individuals provide.

If you intend to observe or talk to people several different times over the course of the program, the choice of respondents will be partially dependent on your time frame. The next section discusses your choice of times and events to measure.

When to look. Time will be important to your sampling plan if the answer to any of these questions is yes:

—Does the program have phases or units that your implementation study should describe separately?
—Do you wish to look at the program periodically in order to monitor whether program implementation is on schedule?
—Do you intend to collect data from any individual site more than once?
—Do you have reason to believe that the program will change over the course of the evaluation?
—If so, do you want to write a profile of the program throughout its history that describes how it evolved or changed?

In these situations, you will probably have to collect data on several different occasions and will need to plan for choosing these times. First, divide the time span of the program into crucial segments, such as beginning, middle, and end; first week, eighth week, thirteenth week; or Topics 1, 3, and 6. You will want to collect information during each of these segments. Then decide from whom and how you will gather information, how you will sample respondents, and whether you will use the same sample of people at each time period or whether you will set up a different sample each time.

If and when you use different samples at different times, be sure to return to the pool the sites or individuals selected to provide data during one particular time segment so that they may be chosen again during a subsequent time segment. People (or sites) should not be eliminated from the pool because they have already provided data. Only when you sample from the *entire* group can you claim that your sample is random and that the information is representative of the entire group.

The timing of your data collection will depend on your evaluation questions and on the specific data collection methods you use. You can administer questionnaires and interviews that ask about typical practice at any time during the period sampled. Some instruments, though, will make it necessary to carefully select or sample particular occasions. If you want your observations, for instance, to record typical events over the course of a typical program day, the records you collect should not come from a period when atypical factors—such as a union strike or flu epidemic—are affecting the program or its participants. Sampling of specific occasions—days, weeks, or possibly even hours—will be necessary as well if you plan to distribute self-report measures that ask respondents to report about what they did "today" or at a specific time or how they felt in response to a specific program activity.

Figure 1 demonstrates how selection of sites, people, and times can be combined to produce a sampling plan for data collection. In Figure 1, a company evaluator has selected sites, people (roles), and times in order to observe a training program in session. The sampling method is useful because, in essence, the evaluator wants to "pull" representative events randomly from the ongoing life of the program. The evaluation strategy is to construct an implementation description from short visits to each of the four sites taking part in the program.

Figure 1 is an example of an extensive sampling strategy; the evaluator chose to look a little at a lot of places. Sampling can be intensive as well—it can look a lot at a few places or people. In such a situation, data from a few sites, classrooms, or students are assumed to mirror that of the whole group. If the set of sites or students is relatively homogeneous—that is, alike in most characteristics that will affect how the program is implemented—you can randomly select representatives and collect as much data as possible from them exclusively. If the program will reach heterogeneous sites, classrooms, or groups, then you should select a representative sample from each category addressed by the program—for instance, clinics in middle-class areas versus clinics in poorer areas; or fifth-grade classes with delinquency-prone students

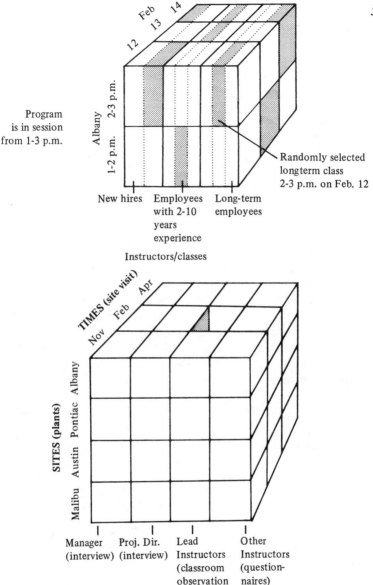

Figure 1. Cubes depicting a sampling plan for measuring implementation of a training program in four sites within a company. The large 4 × 4 × 3 cube shows the overall data-collection plan from which sample cells may be drawn. The smaller cube shows selection of a random sample (shaded segments) of classes and times chosen at the Albany plant for observation during a 3-day February site visit.

versus fifth-grade classes with average students. Then closely examine data from each of these representatives. The strategy of looking intensively at a few places or people is almost always a good idea whether or not you use extensive sampling as well. These intensive studies can form mini-case studies that can help everyone better understand the totality of what is happening in a program.

Step 4. Thinking about validity and reliability

One important consideration in your planning is the technical adequacy of the implementation measures you choose—the validity and reliability of methods used to assess program implementation. Even if you are not a statistical whiz, you should make sure that the instruments you eventually use will help you produce an accurate and complete description of the program you are evaluating. Assessments of the validity and reliability of a measurement instrument help to determine the amount of faith people should place in its results. Validity and reliability refer to different aspects of a measure's credibility. Judgments of *validity* answer the question, *Is the instrument appropriate for what need to be measured?* Judgments of *reliability* answer the question, *Does the instrument yield consistent results?* These are questions you must ask about any method you select to back up your description of program implementation.

Validity has the same root as "valor" and "value"; it indicates how worthwhile a measure is likely to be for telling you what you need to know. Validity boils down to whether the instrument is giving you the true story, or at least something approximating the truth. You are measuring, rather than simply describing the program on the basis of what someone says it looks like, because you want to be able to back up what you say. You are trying to assure both yourself and your audience that the description is an accurate representation of the program as it took place. Such acceptance requires that you anticipate the potential arguments a skeptic might use to dismiss your results. When program implementation is being measured, the most frequent argument made by someone skeptical of your description might go something like this:

> Respondents to an implementation questionnaire or subjects of an observation have an idea of what the program is supposed to look like regardless of whether this is in fact what they usually do. Because they do not wish to appear to deviate or because they fear reprisals, they will bend their responses or behavior to conform to a model of how they feel they ought to appear.

Where this happens, the instrument, of course, will not measure the true implementation of the program. Such an instrument will be invalid.

In measuring program implementation, concern over instrument validity boils down to a four-part question: Is the description of the program which the instrument presents *accurate, relevant, representative,* and *complete?* An *accurate* instrument allows the evaluation audience to create for themselves a picture of a program that is close to what they would have gained had they actually seen the program themselves. A *relevant* implementation measure calls attention to the most critical features of the program—those that are most likely related to the program's outcomes and that someone wishing to replicate the program would be most interested in knowing about. A *representative* description of program implementation will present a typical depiction of the program and its sundry variations as they appeared across sites and over time. A *complete* picture of the program is one that includes all relevant and important program features.

Making a case for accuracy and relevance. You can defend the accuracy of your depiction of the program by ruling out charges that there will be purposeful bias or distortion in the information. There are various ways to guard against such charges. Self-report instruments, for example, can be anonymous. If you will be using observations, you can demonstrate that the observers have nothing to gain by a particular outcome and that the events they witness are not contrived for their benefit. Records kept over the course of the program are particularly easy to defend on this account if they are complete and are checked periodically against the program events they record. You will need to show only that the people extracting the information from the records are unbiased.

You can, in addition, show that administration procedures will be standardized—that is, that the instrument will be used in the same way every time. Make sure of these two points:

—Enough time will be allowed to respondents, observers, or recorders so that the use of the instrument will not be rushed.
—Pressure to respond in a particular way will be absent from the instrument's format and instructions, from the setting of its administration, and from the personal manner of the administrator.

Another way to argue that your description will be accurate is to check that results from any one of your instruments coincide logically with results from other implementation measures.

You can also add support to the accuracy of your instrument by presenting evidence that it is *reliable*. Though it is usually difficult to demonstrate statistically that an implementation instrument is reliable, a good case for reliability can be based on the instrument's having several items that examine each of the program's most critical features. Measuring something important—say, the amount of time participants spend per day working on problems—by means of one item only, exposes your report to potential error from response formulation and interpretation. You can correct this by including several items whose results can be combined to compile an index or by administering the item several times to the same person.

If experts feel that a profile produced by an implementation instrument hits major features of the program you intend to describe, then this is strong evidence that your data will be relevant. For instance, a classroom description would need to include the curriculum used, the amount of time spent on instruction per unit per day, and so forth. A districtwide program, on the other hand, might need to focus heavily on the key administrative arrangements made for the program.

Making a case for representativeness and completeness. To demonstrate representativeness and completeness, you must show that in administering the instrument you will not omit any sites or time periods in which program implementation might look different. You must also show that you will not give too much emphasis to a single atypical variation of the program. Thus your data must sample program sites typical of each of the different places where the program will be implemented. Your sample should also account for different times of the day or different times during the life of the program if these are variations likely to be of concern. The variations you are able to detect must represent the range of those that may occur.

As you can see, there is no one established method for determining validity. Any combination of the types of evidence described here can be used to support validity. If you plan to use an implementation instrument more than once, consider the whole period of its use an opportunity to collect information about the accuracy of the picture it gives you. Each administration is a chance to collect the opinions of experts, to assess the consistency of the view that this instrument gives you with that from other instruments, and so on. Establishing instrument validity should be a continuing process.

Reliability refers to the extent to which measurement results are free of unpredictable kinds of error. For example, if you were to give students a Spanish test one day and, without additional instruction, give them the same test two days later, you would expect each student to receive more or less the same score. If this should turn out not to be the case, you would have to conclude that your instrument is unreliable, because, without instruction, a person's knowledge of Spanish does not fluctuate much from day to day. If the score fluctuates, the problem must be with the test. Its results must be influenced by things other than Spanish knowledge. These other things are called error.

When reliability is used to describe a measurement instrument, it carries the same meaning as when it is used to describe friends. A reliable friend is one on whom you can count to behave the same way time and again. In this sense, an observation instrument, questionnaire, or interview schedule that gives you essentially the same results when readministered in the same setting is a reliable instrument. But while reliability refers to consistency, consistency does not guarantee truthfulness. A friend, for instance, who compliments your taste in clothes each time he sees you is certainly reliable, but may not necessarily be telling the truth. Further, he may not even be deliberately misleading you. Paying compliments may be a habit, or perhaps his judgment of how you dress may be positively influenced by other good qualities you possess. It may be that by a more objective standard you and your friend both have terrible taste in clothes!

Sources of error that affect the reliability of tests, questionnaires, and interviews include the following:

— fluctuations in the mood or alertness of respondents because of illness, fatigue, recent good or bad experiences, or other temporary differences among members of the group being measured
— variations in the conditions of use from one administration to the next, ranging from various distractions (such as unusual outside noises) to inconsistencies and oversights in giving directions
— differences in scoring or interpreting results, chance differences in what an observer notices, and error in computing scores
— random effects caused by examiners or respondents who guess or check off alternatives without trying to understand them

Methods for demonstrating an instrument's reliability—whether the instrument is long and intricate or composed of a single question— usually involve comparing the results of one administration of the instrument with another by correlating them.

The evaluator designing and using instruments for measuring program implementation has unique problems when attempting to demonstrate reliability. Most of these problems stem from the fact that implementation instruments aim at characterizing a situation rather than measuring some quality of a person. While a person's skill in, for example, basic math, can be expected to stay constant long enough for assessment of test reliability to take place, a program cannot be expected to hold still so that it can be measured. Because a program is likely to be dynamic rather than static, possibilities for test-retest and alternate form reliability are usually ruled out. And since most instruments used for measuring implementation are actually collections of single items that independently measure different things, the possibility of computing split-half reliabilities practically never occurs.

Few program evaluators have the luxury of sufficient time to design and validate data collection measures. But early attention to the validity and, to a lesser extent, the reliability of measures will help ensure that information gathered during the evaluation will enable the evaluator to answer well the questions that potential users care about most. An implementation evaluation can be a waste of time if it collects data that are technically "good" but do not answer the right questions. Perhaps worse is the evaluation that relies on data that are weak at best. When decision makers use bad data to guide program decisions, evaluation has done a disservice.

Step 5. Planning for data analysis

People inexperienced in the ways of program evaluation might think that a section devoted to data analysis this early in the book is surely misplaced. But ask anyone who has blithely or blindly collected data before reflecting on how they will be analyzed to detail the potential frustration in completing a study only to realize that the data are either inappropriate for the required analyses or incredibly complicated to code and use. Hours of labor—and perhaps the value of your entire evaluation—can be saved by planning your data analysis or at least thinking about it at this point in your preparations.

You should consider planning in three areas. First, you may well want to skip ahead to Chapter 7 in this book and skim the section on how to prepare data summary sheets. Preparing these now may help you see appropriate changes in the data you need to collect. Second, you may want to check on the availability of computer scoring and analysis using various statistical packages for both mainframe and microcomputers. Third, it may be a good idea to ask a nearby research methodologist or statistician about the appropriateness of your plan and your proposed approach to data analysis. Again, your ability to change what you will do at this point in the evaluation is great; the further you proceed down your time line, the more difficult it is to backtrack and make essential changes. When you have convinced yourself that the data analysis you are proposing is, in fact, feasible and useful, you are ready to begin data collection.

Summary

By the time you have finished working with this chapter, you will have completed five important parts in the planning of your implementation evaluation. First, you will have chosen data collection methods. Second, you will have located appropriate measures if they exist and are readily available. If none are available, you will have thought about exactly what it is you need to collect data about. Third, you will have determined a sampling strategy for your study. Fourth, you will have considered issues related to the validity and reliability of your instruments. And finally, you will have prepared in a general sense for the data analysis that you will eventually face. At this point, then, the planning process is well along, and, with the framework you have created by now, you are ready to move to the specifics of planning detailed in Chapters 4 through 6.

For Further Reading

Fitz-Gibbon, C. T. (1987). *How to analyze data.* Newbury Park, CA: Sage.
Fitz-Gibbon, C. T., & Morris, L. L. (1987). *How to design a program evaluation.* Newbury Park, CA: Sage.
Hays, W. L. (1981). *Statistics* (3rd ed.). New York: Holt, Rinehart & Winston.
Jaeger, R. (1983). *Statistics: A spectator sport.* Newbury Park, CA: Sage.
Mark, M. M., & Cook, T. D. (1984). Design of randomized experiments and quasi-experiments. In L. Rutman (Ed.), *Evaluation research methods* (pp. 65-120). Newbury Park, CA: Sage.
Sudman, S. (1976). *Applied sampling.* New York: Academic Press.

Note

1. Where possible, including a few comparable sites that have not installed the program at all will give you a basis for interpreting some of the data you collect. This will help you determine, for example, whether the absentee rate in the program is unusual or how much added effort is required from instructors. You can gather similar comparison data by monitoring or asking about usual practice at the program sites before the program was initiated.

Chapter 4
Methods for Assessing Program Implementation: Program Records

A historian studying the activities of the past relies in large part on primary sources, documents created at the time in question that, taken together, allow the scholar to recreate a developmental picture of what happened. Evaluators, too, can take advantage of the historian's methods by using a program's records—the tangible remains of program occurrences—to construct a credible portrait of what has gone on in the program. Unobtrusive measures—methods of data-collection that, because they are ongoing or require little effort on any one person's part—can provide valuable information concerning program implementation. Consider the list of commonly kept records given in Table 4. Any of these could be used to develop your description of a program implementation, although you will most likely find the clearest overall picture of the program in those records that program staff have kept systematically on an ongoing basis.

If you want to measure program implementation by means of records, consider two things:

— How can you make good use of *existing* records?
— Can you *set up* a record-keeping system that will give you needed information without burdening the staff?

Where records are already being kept, you can use them as a source of information about the activities they are intended to record. However, since the progress charts, attendance records, enrollment forms, and the like kept for the program will seldom cover all you need to know, you may need to arrange for the staff or participants to record additional information. Of course, you will be able to set up record keeping only if

TABLE 4
Examples of Existing Records

- Certificates upon completion of activities
- Completed student workbooks
- Dog-eared and worn textbooks
- Products produced by students (e.g., drawings, lab reports, poems, essays)
- Attendance and enrollment logs
- Sign-in and sign-out sheets
- Progress charts and checklists
- Unit or end-of-chapter tests
- Teacher-made tests
- Circulation files kept on books and other materials
- Diplomas and transcripts
- Report cards
- Letters of recommendation
- Activity or field-trip rosters
- Letters to and from parents, business persons, the community
- Logs, journals, and diaries kept by students, teachers, or aides
- Parental permission slips
- In-house memos
- Flyers announcing meetings
- Records of bookstore or cafeteria purchases or sales
- Legal documents (e.g., licenses, insurance policies, rental agreements, leases)
- Bills, purchase orders, and invoices from commercial firms providing goods and services
- Minutes or tape-recordings of meetings
- Newspaper articles, news releases and photographs
- Standardized test scores (local and state)

your evaluation begins early enough during program implementation to allow for an accurate picture of what has occurred.

In most cases, it is unrealistic to expect that the staff will keep records over the course of the program solely to help *you* gather implementation information, unless these records are easy to maintain (e.g., sign-in sheets) or are useful for the staff's own purposes as well. You will do best if you come up with a valid reason why the staff should keep records and attempt to align your information needs with theirs. You could, for instance, gain access to records by offering a service. For example, by agreeing to write software for a custom-made management information system, the evaluator of an adolescent parenting center structured ongoing data collection of value to him, to his clients, and to any future evaluator. In another instance, an evaluator was able to monitor program implementation at school sites statewide by helping schools write the periodic reports that had to be submitted to the State Department of Education.

Implementation Evaluation Based on
Records That Already Exist

The following is a suggested procedure to help you find and extract pertinent information within the records that already exist in a program.

Step 1. Construct a program characteristics list

Compose a list of materials, activities, or administrative procedures about which you need supporting data. This procedure was detailed in Chapter 2, pages 28 to 39.

Step 2. Find out from the staff or the program director what records have been kept and which of these are available for your inspection

Be sure you are given a complete listing of every record that the program produced, whether or not it was kept at every site. Probe and suggest sources that might have been forgotten. Draw up a list of all records that will be available to you. If part of your task is to show that the program as implemented represents a departure from past or common practice, you might include records kept *before* the program began.

Step 3. Match the lists from steps 1 and 2

For each type of record, try to find a program feature about which the record may give information. Think about whether any particular record may yield evidence of the following:

— the *duration* or *frequency* of a program activity
— the *form* that the activity took (i.e., what it typically looked like; you will find this information only in narrative records such as curriculum manuals and logs, journals, or diaries kept by the participants)
— the extent of student or other participant *involvement* in the activities (attendance, conduct, interest, etc.)

Do not be surprised if you find that few available records will give you the information you need. The program staff have maintained records to fit their own needs; only *sometimes* will these overlap with yours.

Step 4. Prepare a sampling plan for collecting records

General principles for setting up a data collection sampling plan were discussed in Chapter 3. The methods described there direct you either to sample typical *periods* of program operation at diverse sites or to look intensively at selected cases. Were you to use the former method for describing, say, a language arts program, you might ask to see "library sign-in sheets and circulation files for the *fall quarter* at Boynton Junior High" as well as for other items and other places, all randomly chosen. The latter method directs you to focus on a few sites in detail. An intensive study may cause you to choose Boynton as representative of participating junior high schools and to examine its whole program *in addition to* the library component. You could, as well, find your own way to mix the methods.

If part of your program description task involves showing the extent to which the program is a departure from usual practice, you can include in the sample certain sites not receiving the program and use these for comparison.

Step 5. Set up a data collection roster, and plan how you will transfer the data from the records you examine

The data roster for examining records should look like a questionnaire: "How many people used the library during this particular time unit?" "How long did they stay?" "What kinds of books did they check out?" Responses can take the form of tallies or answers to multiple-choice questions.

When data collection is complete, you may still have to transfer it from the multitude of rosters or questionnaires used in the field to single data summary sheets, described in Chapter 7.

Step 6. Where you have been able to identify available records pertinent to certain program activities, obtain access to these records in such a way that you do not inconvenience the program staff

Arrange to pick up the records or copy them, extract the data you need, and return them as quickly and with as little fuss as possible. A member of the evaluation staff should fill out the data summary sheet; *program* staff should not be asked to transfer data from records to a summary sheet.

Setting Up a Record-Keeping System

What follows is a suggested procedure for establishing a record-keeping system or what is sometimes called management information system (MIS). With the growing availability of computers for even small organizations, program personnel increasingly have the capacity to collect and maintain data for use on an ongoing basis. While evaluators seldom have the luxury of building provisions for their own record keeping into the program itself, they should be prepared to take advantage of such an opportunity if it arises, remembering to structure the record keeping primarily to the needs of program staff and planners and only secondarily to the needs of the implementation evaluation.

Step 1. Construct a program characteristics list for each program you describe

Compose a list of materials, activities, or administrative procedures about which you need supporting data. (This procedure was outlined on pages 28 to 39) If the evaluation uses a control group design or if one of your tasks is to show that the program represents a departure from usual practice, you may need to describe the implementation of more than one program. You should construct a separate list of characteristics for *each* program you describe. Attach to your list, if possible, columns headed in the manner of Columns 2 and 3, Table 5. This table has been constructed to accompany an example illustrating the procedure for setting up a record-keeping system.

Example. Ms. Gregory, Director of Evaluation for a mid-sized school district, is intending to evaluate the implementation of a State-funded compensatory education program for grades K through 3. The program uses individualized instruction. After examining the program proposal and discussing the program with various staff members, she has constructed the implementation record-keeping chart shown in Table 5.

TABLE 5
Example of an Implementation
Record-Keeping Chart

Column 1 Activities (3rd grade)	Column 2 Record to be used for monitoring the activity--adequate for assessing implementation?	Column 3 Frequency and regularity of record collection--sufficiently representative to assess implementation?
1) Early morning warm-up, group exercise (10 min./day)		
2) Individualized reading (45 min./day)		
Each student:		
a) reading aloud with teacher/ aide (3 times/week)		
or		
b) reading cassette work at recorder center (3 times/ week)		
or		
c) reading seatwork--choice of workbook or library book		
3) Perceptual-motor time (15 min. /day in school gym with aide)		
Two parts:		
a) clapping rhythm exercise (in group)		
b) open balance period (individual, on jungle gym, balance beam, etc.)		

Ms. Gregory found that program teachers *already planned* to keep records of students' progress in "reading aloud" (Activity 2a) and of their work with audio tapes in the "recorder corner" (2b). Further this record collection *as planned* seemed to Ms. Gregory to give her exactly the implementation information she needed: teachers planned to monitor reading via a checksheet that would let them note the date of each student's reading session and the number of pages read.

Teachers also planned to note the quality of student performance, a bit of data that Ms. Gregory did *not* need. Work with cassettes in the recorder corner (2b) was to be noted on a special form by an aide, but *only* the progress of children with educational handicaps would be recorded. These audio corner records, Ms. Gregory decided, would not be adequate. She needed data on *all* children's use of the tapes. She noted the usefulness of this information on her chart, with an additional notation to speak to the staff about changing record-keeping in the recorder center to include at least a periodic random sample from the whole class.

Column 1 Activities	Column 2 Record	Column 3 Collection
a) reading aloud with teacher/aide (3 times/week) or	teacher/aide's record book; gives dates of recording, no. of pages read--adequate	constant recording --adequate
b) reading cassette work at recorder center (3 times/week)	aide's recording form; gives amount of time, progress, distractions--adequate	only on EH children --inadequate: speak with staff; could they look at all students?

Ms. Gregory needed some information for which no records were planned. For instance, teachers and aides did not intend to keep records of students' participation in "perceptual-motor time" (Activity 3). Ms. Gregory noted this and determined to meet with the staff to suggest some data collection.

Column 1 Activities	Column 2 Record	Column 3 Collection
3) Perceptual-motor time (15 min. /day in school gym with aide) Two parts:	none--inadequate: suggest that aide keep a checklist or diary of length and content of daily sessions	
a) clapping rhythm exercise (in group)	none--inadequate: aide diary?	
b) open balance period (individual, on jungle gym, balance beam, etc.)	none--inadequate: aide diary?	

Ms. Gregory spoke with aides about the possibility of keeping a diary of perceptual-motor activities. Aides resisted this idea; they wanted the period to be relatively undirected, and they saw it as a break for themselves from regular in-class record-keeping. They did, however, feel that it would be useful to them to have a record of each student's progress in balancing and climbing. Ms. Gregory was thus able to persuade them to construct a checklist called GYM APPARATUS I CAN USE, to be kept by the students themselves and collected once a month. Ms. Gregory decided to collect data on the "clapping" part of the perceptual-motor period in some way other than by examining records, perhaps via a questionnaire to aides at the end of the year, or through observations.

Ms. Gregory was faced with the responsibility of practically single-handedly evaluating a comprehensive year-long program. As it turned out, Ms. Gregory was quite successful at finding records that would provide her with the implementation information she needed. The following records would be made available to her:

- The teachers' record books showing progress in read-aloud sessions
- Aides' recording forms of students' recorder corner work
- Students' GYM APPARATUS I CAN USE checklists

Also available were other records for teaching math, music, and basic science—topic areas not included in the example. All records would be available to Ms. Gregory throughout the year. But how would she find time to extract data from them all?

By means of a time sampling plan, Ms. Gregory could schedule her record collection and data transcription to make the task manageable. First, she chose a *time unit* appropriate for analyzing the types of records she would use. The teachers' records of read-aloud sessions, for example, should be analyzed in *weekly* units rather than daily units. According to Ms. Gregory's activities list, the program did not require students to read every day; they *must* read for the teacher at least three times *per week*. Perceptual-motor time could be analyzed by the day, however, since the program proposal specified a *daily* regimen. She then selected a random sample of *weeks* from the time span of the program and arranged to examine program records at the various sites. She selected *days* for which gym apparatus progress sheets would be examined.

Site and participant selection was random throughout. For each week of data collection, she randomly chose four of the eight participating schools, and within them, two classes per grade whose records would be examined.

Example continued. Having sampled both time units and classrooms, Ms. Gregory consulted teachers' records from eight classrooms at each grade level for the week of January 26. Once she had prepared a list of the 30 students in one of the third grade samples, she

- Tallied the number of times each one read
- Recorded the number of pages read
- Calculated the mean number of pages read that week per student

Ms. Gregory's data roster for gathering information on third-grade read-aloud sessions from one teachers' record book looked like Table 6.

TABLE 6
Example of a Data Roster
for Transferring Information
From Program Records

```
                    Individualized Program

Class:  Mr. Roberts--3rd Grade    School:  Allison Park

Activity:  Reading aloud with     Data source:  Teach-
teacher or aide                   er's record book

Questions:  How often did children read per week?
            How many pages did they cover?

Time Unit:  Week of January 26
```

Student	Tally of times student read		No. of pages read	Mean no. of pages read
Adams, Oliver	////	4	4, 5, 6, 5	5
Ault, Molly	//	2	3, 4	3.5
Caldwell, Maude	///	3	4, 3, 5	4
Connors, Stephen	++++	5	1, 4, 6, 5, 4	4
Ewell, Leo	///	3	3, 5, 4	4
Goldwell, Nora	++++	5	6, 2, 3, 4, 5	4
Gross, Joyce	//	2	7, 8	7.5

Step 2. Find out from the program staff and planners which records will be kept during the program as it is currently planned

Be sure this list includes tests to be given to students, reports to parents, assignment cards—all records that will be produced over the course of the program. Check the availability of the items listed in Table 4.

Step 3. For each program characteristic listed in Step 1, decide if a proposed record can provide information that will be both useful and sufficient for the evaluation's purposes

First, examine the list of records that will be available to you. Will any of them be useful as a check of either quantity, quality, regularity of occurrence, frequency, or duration of the program characteristic? If any record will, enter its name on your activities chart next to the activity whose occurrence it will demonstrate. Jot down a judgment of whether the record *as is* will fit your needs or whether it needs slight modification. Also enter the number of collections or updatings of the record that will take place over the course of the program. If the number of collections seems insufficient to give a good picture of the program, talk to the staff to request more frequent updating.

Step 4. For those characteristics that are *not* covered by the staff's list of planned records, decide if simple additions or alterations can provide appropriate and adequate evaluation data

When you have finished your review of available records, look closely at the set of program activities about which you still need information. These will *not* be covered by the staff's list of planned records. Try to think of ways in which alteration or simple addition to one of the records already scheduled for collection may give you information on the frequency of occurrence or the form of one of the activities on your list. If it appears that slight alteration of a record will give you the information you need, note the name of the record and its planned collection frequency and request that the program staff make the changes you need.

Step 5. Meet with program staff first to review the planned records that will provide data for the evaluation and second to recommend changes and additions for their consideration

Before seriously approaching the staff and asking for their assistance with your information collection plan, however, scrutinize it as follows:

— Will it be too time-consuming for the staff to fill out regularly?
— Will the staff members perceive it as useful to them?
— Can you arrange a feedback system of any sort to give the staff *useful* and *timely* information based on the records you plan to ask them to keep?

If the information plan you have conceived passes these checkpoints, suggest it to the staff.

Try to avoid data overload. Do not produce a mass of data for which there is little use. They way to avoid collecting an unnecessary volume of data is to plan data use *before* data collection.

Step 6. Prepare a sampling plan for collecting records

Once you know which records will be kept to facilitate your implementation evaluation, decide where, when, and from whom you will collect them. General principles for setting up a data collection sampling plan were discussed in Chapter 3. The methods described there produce two types of samples:

— a sample that selects typical time periods or episodes from the program at diverse sites
— a sample that selects people, classes, schools, or other sites, considering each *case* typical of the program

Your sampling plan can use either or both types.

Step 7. Set up a data collection roster and plan how you will transfer data from the records you examine

The data roster for examining records should resemble a questionnaire for which answers take the form of tallies or, in some cases, multiple-choice items. The data roster is a means for making implementation information accessible to you when you need it so that it can be included in the data analysis for your report. The roster, you will notice, compiles information from a *single* source, covering a single time period. For the purpose of your report, you will usually have to transfer all of the roster data to a *data summary sheet* in order to look at the *program as a whole.* Chapter 7 describes data summary sheets, including those for managing data processing by computer.

Step 8. Set up a means for obtaining easy access to the records you need

Gather records from the staff in a way that minimally interferes with their busy work schedules. You or your delegate should arrange to collect workbooks, reports, checklists, or whatever, photocopy them or extract the important data, and return these records as quickly as possible. Only in those rare situations where the staff itself is ungrudgingly willing to participate in your data collection should you ask them to bring records to you or to transfer information to the roster.

Step 9. Check periodically to make sure that the information you have requested from program staff is in fact being recorded accurately and completely

It is one thing for an evaluator to plan an implementation evaluation thoroughly at the beginning of a program. It is another thing altogether to return, say, a year later and actually find the records ready for use. In many cases you may return at the end of the year to discover that what you thought program staff were going to do in the area of record keeping and what they actually did were two different things. If the effectiveness of your evaluation relies on records kept by program personnel, you are well advised to check periodically to make sure that the information you need is being collected and maintained. In the press of program activities, record keeping may become burdensome or, given limited resources, even an inappropriate use of staff time.

For Further Reading

Guba, E. G., & Lincoln, Y. S. (1981). Using documents, records, and unobtrusive measures. In E. G. Guba & Y. S. Lincoln, *Effective evaluation* (pp. 226-269). San Francisco: Jossey-Bass.

Patton, M. Q. (1982). Managing management information systems. In M. Q. Patton, *Practical evaluation* (pp. 227-239). Newbury Park, CA: Sage.

Smith, N. (1981). Document analysis in program evaluation. *NWREL Newsletter, 4*(1).

Weber, R. (1985). Basic content analysis. *Quantitative applications in the social sciences* (Vol. 49). Newbury Park, CA: Sage.

Chapter 5
Methods for Assessing Program Implementation: Questionnaires and Interviews

Chapter 4 described ways in which evaluators can use program records to provide one type of implementation information. Because records are for the most part written documents, however, the picture they create may be incomplete, lacking the details that only those who experienced the program can provide. A good way to find out what a program actually looked like is to ask the people involved. The focus of this chapter, therefore, is *self-reports,* the personal responses of program faculty, staff, administration, and participants.

Self-reports typically take one of two forms: questionnaires and interviews. Questionnaires asking about different individuals' experiences with a program enable one evaluator to collect information efficiently from a large number of people. Individual or group interviews are more time-consuming, but provide face-to-face descriptions and discussion of program experiences. Where there is a plan or theory for the program, gathering information from staff will involve questioning them about the consistency between program activities as they were planned and as they actually occurred. Where the program has not been prescribed, information from people connected with it will describe how the program evolved.

Whether they are questionnaires or interviews, self-reports also differ on the dimension of time. They can consist of either periodic reports throughout the program or retrospective reports after the program has ended. Periodic reports will generally yield more accurate implementation information because they allow respondents to report about program activities soon after they have occurred, when they are still fresh in memory. For this reason, they are nearly always more credible than retrospective reports.

Periodic reports should be used even when your role is summative and you are required to describe the program only once, at its conclusion. Retrospective self-reports should be used in only two cases: when there is no other choice (e.g., because the evaluation is commissioned near the program's conclusion) or when the program is small enough or of such short duration that reconstructions after-the-fact will be believable. What follows are step-by-step directions for collecting self-reports through periodic questionnaires or interviews. These can be adapted easily to develop a retrospective report.

How to Gather Periodic Self-Reports
Over the Course of the Program

Step 1. Decide how many times you will distribute questionnaires or conduct interviews and from whom you will collect self-reports

As soon as you begin working on the evaluation and as early as possible in the program's life, decide how often you will need to collect self-report information. This decision will be determined by three factors:

— *The homogeneity of program activities.* If each program unit has essentially the same format as the others, then you will not need to document descriptions of particular ones. If, for example, a company's program for updating employees' knowledge in a technical field consists of standardized lessons containing lectures, readings, and class discussion, then any one lesson you ask about at any given site will reflect the typical format of the program. In such a case you can plan data collection at your discretion. If, on the other hand, the program has certain unique features—say, group project assignments that will vary from site to site or special guest lectures by local university professors—you will want to ask about these distinguishing program features as soon as they occur. This will give you a chance to digest information and provide immediate formative feedback to program planners and staff.

— *Your assessment of people's tolerance for interruptions.* Unless the program is sparsely staffed, you should not ask for more than three reports from any one individual over the span of a long-term program (e.g., a year). You can *sample,* of course, so that the chances are reduced that any one person will be asked to report often.

— *The amount of time you expect to have available for scoring and interpreting information in reports.*

Once you have decided *when* to collect self-reports, create a sampling strategy (see pages 49 to 54) by deciding whom you will ask for self-report information (both by title and by name) and how you will ensure that various program sites are adequately represented.

Step 2. Alert people that you will be requesting periodic information

As early during the evaluation as possible, inform staff members and others that in order to measure implementation of their program, you must ask that they provide you with information about how the program looks in operation.

Step 3. Construct a program characteristics list

Procedures for listing the characteristics of the program—materials, activities, administrative arrangements—that you will examine are discussed in Chapter 2.

Step 4. Decide, if you have not already, whether to distribute questionnaires, to interview, or to do both

You probably know about the relative advantages and disadvantages of using questionnaires or interviews. Table 3 reminded you of some of them. If you are using self-report instruments to supplement program description data from a more credible source—observations or records—then questionnaire data should be sufficient. On the other hand, if self-report measures will provide your only implementation backup data, then you should interview some participants. Even if you are a clever questionnaire writer, you probably cannot find out all you need to know about the program from a pencil-and-paper instrument. Interviews allow a sensitive evaluator to come face to face with important program concepts and issues.

Step 5. Write questions based on the list from Step 3 that will prompt people to tell you what they saw and did as they participated in the program

Anyone who writes questions or develops items on a regular basis would do well to consult the books listed at the end of this chapter as what can be presented here represents only a small part of available knowledge on how to do this well. The development of good items for questionnaires and interviews clearly combines art, science, common sense, and practice. What follows is a brief summary of things to consider when writing questionnaire or interview items. You should also consult Table

7 for a list of pointers to follow when writing questions for a program implementation instrument.

To begin, one thing you will need to know is how participants used the materials and engaged in the activities that made up the program. To this end, you should ask about three topics:

(1) *The occurrence, frequency, and duration of activities.* Whether you collect frequency and duration information in addition to occurrence data will depend on the program. To describe a science laboratory program, for example, you would need merely to determine whether the planned labs occurred at all—and in the correct sequence. If, on the other hand, the program in question consisted of daily, 45-minute English conversation drills, then you would need to know whether the activity occurred with the prescribed frequency and duration.

(2) *The form the activities took.* Gathering information on the form of the activities means asking about which students took part in the activities, which materials were used and how often, what activities looked like, and possibly where they occurred. It will also be useful to check whether the form of the activities remained constant or whether the activities changed from time to time or from student to student.

(3) *The amount of involvement of participants in these activities.* Besides knowing what activities occurred, you should make some check on the extent of interest and participation on the part of the target group—for example, the students. Even if activities were set up using the prescribed schedule, students can only be expected to have learned from them if the students paid attention to the activities. Were students in a math tutoring program, for instance, mostly working on the prescribed exercises, or were they conversing about sports and clothes some of the time? Were participants actually exploring the enrichment materials during their unstructured time, or were they just doing their homework? Some of this slippage is inevitable in every program, as in all human endeavor. Still, it is important to find out the extent of non-involvement in the program you are evaluating.

If you are designing a questionnaire, then you have a choice of two question formats: closed-response or open-response (also known as selected or constructed, respectively). Ease of scoring and clear reporting lead most evaluators to use closed-response questionnaires. On such a questionnaire, the respondent is asked to check or otherwise indicate a provided answer to a specific question. Recording the answers involves a simple tally of response categories chosen. On the open-response questionnaire, the respondent is asked to write out a short answer to a more general question. The open-response format has the advantage of

TABLE 7
Some Principles To Follow When Writing Questions For An Instrument To Describe Program Implementation

To ensure usable responses to implementation questions:

1. When possible, ask about specific—and recent—events or time periods such as *today's math lesson, Thursday's field trip, last week*. This persuades people to think concretely about information that should still be fresh in memory. To alleviate your own and the respondent's concern about representativeness of the event, ask for an estimate, and perhaps an explanation, of its typicality.

2. When asking a closed-response question, try to imagine what could have gone wrong with the activities that were planned. Use these possibilities as response alternatives. Resourceful anticipation of likely activity changes will affect the usefulness of the instrument for uncovering changes that did indeed occur. If you feel that you cannot adequately anticipate discrepancies between planned and actual activities, then add "other" as a response alternative and ask respondents to explain.

3. Be sure that you do not *answer* the question by the way you ask it. A good question about what people *did* should not contain a suggestion about how to answer. For instance, questions such as "Were there 4th- and 5th-graders in the program?" or "Did you meet every Monday afternoon?" suggest information you should receive from the respondent. Rather, these questions should be phrased, "What were the grade levels of the students in the program?" "What days of the week and how regularly did you meet?"

4. Identify the frame of reference of the respondents. In an interview, you can learn a great deal from how a person responds as well as from what he says; but when you use a questionnaire, your information will be limited to written responses. The *phrasing* of the questions will therefore be critical. Ask yourself:

   • *What vocabulary would be appropriate to use with this group?*
   • *How well informed are the respondents likely to be?* Sometimes people are perfectly willing to respond to a questionnaire, even when they know little about the subject. They feel they are *supposed* to know, otherwise you would not be asking them. To allow people to express ignorance gracefully, you might include lack of knowledge as a response alternative. Word the alternative so that it does not demean the respondent, for instance, "I have not given much thought to this matter."
   • *Does the group have a particular perspective that must be taken into account—a particular bias?* Try to see the issue through the eyes of the respondents before you begin to ask the questions.

allowing respondents to freely give information you have not antici-
pated, but it is time-consuming to score; and unless you have available a
large number of readers, it is not practical for any but the smallest
evaluations. Most questionnaires ask principally closed-response questions, but add a few open-response options. These allow respondents to
volunteer information important to the evaluation but not specifically
requested.

To demonstrate how different question types result in different
information, Figures 2, 3, and 4 present combinations of open- and
closed-response questions for collecting implementation information
on the same program. Figure 2 is entirely open-ended; Figure 3
combines open- and closed-ended questions; and Figure 4 uses a closed-
response format exclusively. While the data that would result from the
questionnaire in Figure 4 would be easily analyzed, this ease is gained at
the expense of the more detailed information that individual teachers
might write in on the two other questionnaire formats. The appropriateness of the questionnaire items finally selected will depend both on
the questions asked in the evaluation as a whole and on the availability
of evaluation staff to analyze open-response format items. In general, it
is worth including at least one open-ended question on every questionnaire, whether or not the results will later be reported. Giving people an
opportunity to write down their concerns alerts them to the importance
of their perspective and provides the evaluation helpful information for
guiding program activities.

Like questionnaires, *interviews* can also take several forms, again
depending on how questions are asked. Interviews can range from
informal personal conversations with program personnel at one extreme,
to highly quantitative interviews that consist of a respondent and an
evaluator completing a closed-response format questionnaire together
at the other extreme.[1]

A basic distinction can be made between interviews that are
structured and those that are unstructured. In a structured interview, an
evaluator asks specific questions in a predetermined order. Neither the
questions nor their order is varied across interviewers, and in its purest
form the interviewer's job is merely to ask the prespecified questions and
to record the responses. In cases where an evaluator already has ideas
about how a program looked, structured interviews can readily provide
corroboration and supporting data.

By contrast, an unstructured interview can explore areas of implementation that were either unplanned or evolved differently from the

DOCUMENTATION QUESTIONNAIRE

Peer-Tutoring Program

The following are questions about the peer-tutoring program implemented this year. We are interested in knowing your opinions about what the program looked like in operation. Please respond to each question, and feel free to write additional information on the back of this questionnaire.

(1) How was the peer-tutoring program structured in your classroom?

(2) How were tutors selected?

(3) How were students selected for tutoring?

(4) What materials seemed to work best in the peer-tutoring sessions? Why?

(5) What were the strengths of the peer-tutoring program this year?

(6) What changes would you make to improve the program next year?

Figure 2. Example of an open-response questionnaire

DOCUMENTATION QUESTIONNAIRE
Peer-Tutoring Program

The following are statements about the peer-tutoring program implemented this year. We are interested in knowing whether they represent
an accurate statement of what the program looked like in operation.
For this reason, we ask that you indicate, using the 1 to 5 scale
after each statement, whether it was "generally true," etc. Please
circle your answer. If you answer seldom or never true, please use
the lines under the statement to correct its inaccuracy.

	always true	gener-ally true	seldom true	never true	don't know
1. Students were tutored three times a week for periods of 45 minutes each.	1	2	3	4	5
2. Tutoring took place in the classroom, tutors working with their own classmates.	1	2	3	4	5
3. Tutors were the fast readers.	1	2	3	4	5
4. Students were selected for tutoring on the basis of reading grades.	1	2	3	4	5
5. Tutoring used the "Read and Say" workbooks.	1	2	3	4	5
6. There were no discipline problems.	1	2	3	4	5

Figure 3. An example of a questionnaire that uses
both closed- and open-response formats

```
                         DOCUMENTATION QUESTIONNAIRE
                            Peer-Tutoring Program

Please answer the following questions by placing the letter of the
most accurate response on the line to the left of the question.  We
are interested in finding out what the project looked like in opera-
tion during the past week, regardless of how it was planned to look.
If more than one answer is true, answer with as many letters as you
need.

_____   1.  On the average, how many times did tutoring sessions take
             place in your classroom?

             a) never                    c) 3 or 4 times

             b) 1 or 2 times             d) 5 or more times

_____   2.  What was the average length of a tutoring session?

             a) 5-15 minutes            c) 25-45 minutes

             b) 15-25 minutes           d) longer than 45 minutes

_____   3.  Where in the school did tutoring usually take place?

             a) classroom               c) library

             b) sometimes classroom,    d) room other than classroom
                sometimes other room       or library

_____   4.  Who were the tutors?

             a) only fast students      c) only average students

             b) fast students and some  d) other
                average students

_____   5.  On what basis were tutees selected?

             a) reading achievement     c) general grade average

             b) teacher recommendations d) other

_____   6.  What materials were used by teachers and tutors?

             a) whatever tutors chose   c) "Read and Say" workbooks

             b) specially constructed    d) other
                games

_____   7.  How typical of the program as a whole was last week, as you
             have described it here?

             a) just the same           c) some aspects not typical

             b) almost the same         d) not typical at all
```

Figure 4. Example of a closed-response questionnaire

plan.[2] In an unstructured interview the evaluator poses a few general questions and then encourages respondents to amplify their answers. The unstructured interview is more like a conversation and does not necessarily follow a specific question sequence. Unstructured interviews require considerable interviewing skill. General questions for the unstructured interview can be phrased in several ways. Consider the following questions:

— How often, how many times, or how many hours a week did the program (or its major features) occur?
— What can you tell me about how the activities actually looked—can you recall an instance and describe to me exactly what went on?
— How involved did the students seem to be—did all students participate, or were there some students who were always absent or distracted?
— I understand that you are attempting to implement a behavior modification (open classroom, quality circle, whatever) program here. What kinds of activities have been suggested to you by this point of view?

Since unstructured interviews resemble conversations and can easily go off track, they require not only that you compose a few questions to stimulate talk but also that you write and use *probes*. Probes are short comments to stimulate the respondent to say or remember more and to guide the interview toward relevant topics. These are two frequently used probes:

— Can you tell me more about that?
— Why do you think that happened?

There is no set format for probes. In fact, a good way of probing to gain more complete information from respondents who may have forgotten or left something out of their answer might be a simple "I see. Is there anything else?" You should insert probes whenever the respondent makes a strong statement in either an expected or an unexpected direction. For instance, a teacher might say, "Oh yes. Participation, student involvement was very high—100%." The best probe for such a strong response is simple rephrasing and repetition: "Your statement is that every student participated 100% of the time?" This probe leads the respondent to reconsider.

Step 6. Assemble the questionnaire or interview instrument

Arrange questions in a logical order. Do not ask questions that jump from one subject to another. Compose an introduction. The introduction honors the respondents' right to know why they are being questioned. *Questionnaire* instructions should be specific and unambiguous. Aim for as simple a format as possible. You should assume that a portion of the respondents will ignore instructions altogether. If you feel the format may be confusing, include a conspicuous sample item at the beginning. Instructions for a mailed questionnaire should mention a *deadline* for its return, and, to increase return rates, you should enclose a self-addressed, stamped envelope.

Instructions for an *interview* can be more detailed, of course, and should include reassurances to allay the respondent's initial apprehension about being questioned. Specifically, the interviewer should do the following:

— *State the purpose of the interview.* Explain what organization you represent and why you are conducting the evaluation. Explain the purpose of the interview. Describe the report you will have to make regarding the activities that occurred in the program; explain if possible how the information the respondent gives you might affect the program.

— *State whether or not the respondent's statement can be kept confidential.* In situations where a social or professional threat to the respondent may be involved, confidentiality of interviews must be stressed and strictly maintained.

— *Explain to the respondent what will be expected during the interview.* For instance, if it will be necessary for the respondent to go back to the classroom to get records, explain why.

Some of the above information should probably be made available to questionnaire respondents as well. This can be done by including a cover letter with the questionnaire.

Step 7. Try out the instrument

Before administering or distributing any instrument, check it out. Give it to one or two people to read aloud, and observe their responses. Have the people explain to you their understanding of what each question is asking. If the questions are not interpreted as you intended, alter them accordingly.

Always rehearse the interview. Whether you choose to prepare a structured or unstructured interview, once the questions for the interview are selected the interview should be rehearsed. You and other interviewers should run through it once or twice with whoever is available—a spouse, an older child, a colleague. This dry run is a test of both the instrument and interviewer. Look for inconsistency in the logic of the question sequence and for questions that are difficult to understand or sound threatening. Advise the person who is playing the role of respondent to be as uncooperative as possible to prepare interviewers for unanticipated answers and even hostility.

Step 8. Administer the instrument according to the sampling plan from Step 1

If you *mail questionnaires,* give respondents about two weeks to return them. Then follow up with a reminder, a second mailing or a phone call if possible. How do you do such a follow up if people are to respond anonymously? One procedure is to number the return envelopes, check them off a master list as they are returned, remove the questionnaires from the envelope, and throw the envelopes away. When distributing any instrument, ask administrators to lend their support. If the instrument carries the sanction of the project director or the school principal, it is more likely to receive the attention of those involved. The superintendent's request for quick returns will carry more authority than yours.

If you *interview,* consider the following suggestions:

— Interviewers should be aware of their influence over what respondents say. Questions about the administration of the program may make them look bad in a report. Explain to the respondents that the report will refer to no one personally. Understand, as well, that respondents will speak more candidly to interviewers whom they perceive as being like themselves—not representatives of authority.
— Interviewers should have a plan for dealing with reluctant respondents. The best way to overcome resistance is to be explicit about the interview and what it will demand of the respondent.
— If possible, interviews—particularly unstructured ones—should be recorded on audiotape to be transcribed at a later time. Recorded interviews enable you to summarize the information using exact quotations from the respondent; the obvious drawback is that they also require a great deal of transcription time. Transcribing the tape in full will take two to three times as long as the interview itself. An alternative is that interviewers take notes during an unstructured interview. Notes should include a general summary of each response, with key phrases recorded verbatim. If possible summaries of unstructured interviews should be returned to respondents so that misunderstandings in the transcription can be corrected.

Step 9. Record data from questionnaires and interview instruments on a data summary sheet

Chapter 7 will describe the use of a data summary sheet for recording data from many forms in one place. Data from closed-response items on questionnaires and structured interview forms can be transferred directly to the data summary sheet or can be entered directly onto a computer tape or file. Responses to open-response items and unstructured interviews will have to be summarized before they can be further interpreted. Procedures for reducing a large amount of narrative information by either summarizing or quantifying it will be discussed in Chapter 7. Even if you plan to write a narrative report of your results, the data summary sheet will show trends in the data that can be described in the narrative.

Notes

1. Because this quantitative interview format does not take advantage of the face-to-face interaction between evaluator and respondent, it is more properly considered the enactment of a questionnaire rather than an interview.

2. For more information on unstructured interviews, see *How to Use Qualitative Methods in Evaluation* (Volume 4 of the *Program Evaluation Kit*).

For Further Reading

Bradburn, N. M., & Sudman, S. (1979). *Improving interview methodology and questionnaire design.* San Francisco: Jossey-Bass.

Converse, J. M., & Presser, S. (1986). Survey questions: Handcrafting the standardized questionnaire. *Quantitative applications in the social sciences* (Vol. 63). Newbury Park, CA: Sage.

Fowler, F. J. (1984). *Survey research methods.* Newbury Park, CA: Sage.

Henerson, M. E., Morris, L. L., & Fitz-Gibbon, C. T. (1987). *How to measure attitudes.* Newbury Park, CA: Sage.

Patton, M.Q. (1987). *How to use qualitative methods in evaluation.* Newbury Park, CA: Sage.

Payne, S. L. (1951). *The art of asking questions.* Princeton, NJ: Princeton University Press.

Sudman, S., & Bradburn, N. M. (1982). *Asking questions: A practical guide to questionnaire design.* San Francisco: Jossey-Bass.

Chapter 6
Methods for Assessing Program Implementation: Observations

Most audiences consider the observations of people who are not staff members highly credible sources of information about program implementation, and for obvious reasons. Reports of observers are based on what people have *directly seen* while observing the program in operation. They have witnessed participants talking with teachers and working with program materials; they have explored the instructional setting or attended planning meetings; they have experienced a live enactment of the program. What is more, since they probably have nothing to gain from depicting the program in any particular way, they will rarely be charged with bias.

Because of the credibility and richness of the information it can provide, on-site observation is often a desirable part of an implementation evaluation. Of all implementation measures, observation places the evaluator closest to the operation of the program. Some evaluators feel, in fact, that observation is the only method for capturing and aptly describing a program's complexity because formal observations take a long look at representative parts of the program and record accurately what is seen.

Planning to Observe:
First Considerations

The simplest and most common type of observation is informal, the personal reaction of an outsider seeing a program in progress. Whether or not the formal plan includes observation as an evaluation activity, evaluators cannot help but witness program events during the course of an evaluation. They may come to administer questionnaires and watch five minutes of class before the instructor turns the group over to them.

They may attend staff meetings and, by chance, observe interactions among key program figures. They may tour program facilities and, in so doing, casually observe several different classrooms.

Such informal observations are important because they give the evaluator a sense of context, an intuitive feeling for a program's implementation. These casual, informal observations, however, are not the topic of this chapter because, from a technical standpoint, *unsystematic* observations are not rigorous enough to be included as evaluation data. Informal observation procedures are always open to the challenge of the skeptical audience that might say,

— The people observing weren't prepared, so they didn't know what to look for.
— See—even they misinterpreted what we were doing.
— They came at the wrong time and didn't stay long enough.

Unfortunately, in recent discussions of the value of qualitative methods, persons only superficially aware of the techniques have claimed that casual observations of this type somehow represent qualitative evaluation methods. But it is simply not the case that any evaluation information that cannot be typed into a computer as numerical data has necessarily resulted from a qualitative approach. Information gathered informally and casually may be highly useful, but it should make no claim to scientific rigor, either quantitative *or* qualitative.

Instead, it is helpful to picture a range of possible approaches to program observation on a continuum from the highly structured approach typically connected with traditional research to what can be an equally systematic approach that allows critical issues to emerge during the course of observations. At one end of the continuum, evaluators determine the categories and questions of interest in advance. They are careful to prescribe *what* and *when* observers watch and *how they record* what they see. They often make use of disinterested third party observers, people who have no stake in the implementation evaluation's findings.

At the other end of the continuum, evaluators may observe or even become actively involved in the program over time, using observation and other forms of systematic information gathering (e.g., periodic questionnaires or interviews). Their analysis of field data is ongoing so that the questions they focus on are generated from the implementation and, at the same time, the data they collect can provide answers to these questions (for further discussion, see *How to Use Qualitative Methods in Evaluation*, Volume 4 of the *Program Evaluation Kit*).

Regardless of the overall design of the evaluation, observations demand careful planning and training of observers. If you intend to gather implementation information using observations, then your first task will be to decide if you will determine *in advance* what will be observed and how, or if, instead, you will become involved in the program and use observation methods to look systematically for matters of importance to program staff. This decision, like others in evaluation, will depend in part on your role with regard to the program—whether you are to summarize it or to help in its development; your need for credibility; and the relative size of the project. If you opt for the second approach, you would do well at this point to read *How to Use Qualitative Methods in Evaluation* (Volume 4 of the *Program Evaluation Kit*).

Is one approach to observation necessarily better or more "scientific" than another? The answer is a resounding "no"; the quality of observation depends not on the given approach itself but rather on two things: (1) the appropriateness of its use in a specific evaluation setting; and (2) the rigor with which it is applied. *Any* observation plan that is inappropriate or poorly implemented will be a waste of time and often of scarce resources.

Making Formal Observations

The procedures in this section are organized according to the following 12 steps that outline an approach for making formal observations:

(1) Construct a program characteristics list describing how the program is supposed to look.
(2) Prepare scenarios of typical program episodes.
(3) Prepare scenarios of episodes that should not occur.
(4) Choose an observation method.
(5) Decide how long each observation time sample must be in order to yield good data and determine how many time samples are needed.
(6) Prepare a sampling plan for conducting observations.
(7) Prepare the observers' recording sheets.
(8) Choose observers.
(9) Train observers and document inter-rater reliability.
(10) Inform the program staff about the upcoming observations.
(11) Conduct observations for the time samples you have chosen from the program's duration.
(12) When observation data are in, score them and prepare them for interpretation and presentation.

Before you become embroiled in designing your own observation system, you would do well to look around for one you might adapt, perhaps one that has been used with similar programs. Pages 109 to 112, for example, describe an observation scheme created at the Stanford Research Institute. It is a good model for observation instruments that record what occurs during class sessions. You might check as well some of the observation instruments you can locate through the sources listed in Chapter 3 and in the "For Further Reading" section at the end of this chapter.

The first four steps of the procedure outlined below are intended to help you decide *what to look for*. If you already know what you want or need to examine, you can begin developing your observation procedure at Step 5. You may, however, want to read over the first four steps to check that you have not overlooked something.

Step 1. Construct a program characteristics list

Compose a list of materials, activities, and/or administrative procedures about which you need supporting data. This task, which includes visiting program sites, if possible, to see the program in operation, is outlined in Chapter 2. The completed list serves two functions: it gives you an outline of what the program should ideally look like; and it enables you to point to the key materials and arrangements of facilities that should be present and the activities that should be occurring.

Step 2. Prepare scenarios of typical program episodes

Scenarios are short descriptions of the actions and interactions exhibited by teachers, students, or other participants when the program as planned is in operation. Augmenting the list composed in Step 1, the scenarios build a foundation for designing a systematic observation scheme by helping to define what these program activities might look like when they occur. Where the scenario includes terms that imply specific actions, these should be defined. A scenario may stipulate, for instance, that teachers direct positive or reinforcing comments to students. You will need to define these terms clearly enough so that observers can agree about which teacher statements are reinforcing or positive and which are not. If the scenario mentions student play behaviors, you will have to instruct your observers about what "play" looks like. Should, for example, work with math-related materials *not* assigned by the teacher be classified as play or as math instruction? Similarly, you may need to define attentive versus inattentive behaviors.

Figure 5 shows a scenario for a typical lesson in a phonics-based reading program for the first grade. The scenario outlines four aspects of the program:

— The features of the space, in this case the classroom; in another case it could be a hospital ward, an auditorium, or whatever. A scenario might include, as well, a sketch of the layout of the typical place in which observations will occur—if aspects of its arrangement are important to the program.

— Characterization of the materials and other objects relevant to the program that are present. Note that the flash cards in the example are described in terms of both content and use.

— A list of the people involved. The figure notes that the lesson would usually be conducted by the teacher and that an aide is rare.

— Narrative depiction of the activities in which people are taking part. This depiction is both general and specific. The *general* depiction describes the actions of groups of people over a considerable duration of time. For example, reading rotates from child to child until the story is finished. *Specific* activities describe the words or gestures of individuals at a certain time. For example, when a child makes an error reading a word, the teacher initiates the sounding and blending procedure standard to the program.

Step 3. Prepare scenarios of episodes that should not occur

These scenarios will list alternative but undesirable program features. They will describe the most likely ways in which things can go wrong, so that observers can check for their occurrence. The scenario in Figure 6 describes the behaviors that should not occur during the reading instruction lesson described in Figure 5. For example, the teacher should *not* work with fewer than two children; the story should *not* be given a long introduction; and the teacher should *not* omit praise for correct answers.

The three steps just described help you to uncover the critical parts of the program that may be buried in the program proposal or in the theory or model of learning held important by the program's planners and staff. Once you have completed the scenarios, show them to the program planners and staff and ask for their comments. In particular, you should ask them which parts of the program they consider absolutely critical as opposed to those that just would be nice to have. If your function is formative, the staff can tell you which parts they want to monitor. Once you are satisfied that you know which features of the program should be the focus of your observations, you need to choose an observation method.

What the Observers Should Find

1. The classroom. Approximately 30 children are working on individual
   assignments. The teacher and a group of three or four students are
   seated in a circle in one corner of the room for the phonics lesson.

2. Objects and materials. The teacher has a deck of flashcards and a
   primer. Each student has a primer only. The flashcards used by the
   teacher should contain, for review, some previously learned graphemes
   and some recently taught. The deck should contain one or two new
   graphemes or clusters that will appear in the story to be read.

3. People. The primer lesson involves a teacher--or rarely an aide--and
   three or four students. One or two aides supervise students doing
   seatwork.

4. Activities--general. The teacher starts the lesson by showing the
   flashcards one at a time, then questions the students individually
   about the sound made by the vowel, consonant, or cluster showing on
   the card. Individual children are asked to respond. Correct answers
   are praised; when a student gives a wrong answer, the teacher asks
   for volunteers from the group to correct it. After each child has
   had a chance to respond correctly to about three letters or clusters,
   the flashcard section ends and the story is begun.

   After a brief introduction from the teacher, individual students are
   asked to read aloud. Reading errors are treated by the teacher
   through a prompting procedure in which the child is persuaded to
   blend the letters in the word. The reading thus rotates from child
   to child in the group until the story is completed. When the story
   is over, the teacher calls on various students to summarize the main
   points in the story. This group lesson lasts about half an hour;
   each student in the class takes part in this phonics group about
   three times a week.

   Activities--specific. Wrong answers during the flashcard section of
   the lesson elicit a response from the teacher: "No, that's not
   right. Who else would like to try?" or some similar statement. The
   teacher introduces the story with a single sentence. Such a sentence
   hints at the theme of the story; for instance, "This is a story about
   a rabbit with a peculiar habit."

   When a child reading aloud makes an error or stumbles on a word, the
   teacher initiates the sounding and blending procedure standard to the
   program. This procedure is more or less as follows: Teacher--
   "What's the first syllable? Look at the first letter. What sound
   does it make?...Look at the second letter," etc. "Now blend them
   together." If sounding and blending fail to produce the word after
   about 45 seconds, the teacher asks: "What kind of word do you think
   belongs in that place in the sentence? An object word or an action
   word? Can you guess what the word might be?" If this fails also,
   the teacher tells the child the word and demonstrates for him how its
   sound matches its graphic representation.

Figure 5. Scenario of a typical lesson: Phonics Bases
of Reading Program, First Grade, Primer Level

What Observers Should Not See Taking Place

1. The classroom.

2. Objects and materials. Flashcards may not contain more than three new graphemes or clusters (no story in the primer introduces more than two), and the flashcard deck must contain previously learned ones for review and motivation.

3. People. The teacher should not work with fewer than two nor more than five children at one time.

4. Activities--general. The reading of the primer should occur after the flashcard lesson. The flashcard section of the lesson may not conclude until every child has had a chance to make at least two correct responses even if all are with the same letter. The story may not be given a long introduction. This means an introduction of longer than five sentences.

   Activities--specific. Teachers must not ask for the names of letters on the flashcards, only for their sounds. Students who give names should be corrected in the following way: "Yes, but what is its sound?" The teacher should not fail to praise correct answers and must not make prolonged explanatory responses to incorrect answers. Statements such as, "No, Donald, not \e\; the sound is \i\," or "Come on, Nancy, you got that one right last time" are long enough. When readers are having difficulty with a word in the story, the teacher should not suggest that the child look at the picture. Although stick drawings appear in the primer, attention is not to be called to them. When a child is attempting to identify an unknown word, all attention should be called to the printed word and the clues to be gotten from the words in the story.

Figure 6. Scenario of *un*desirable events of Phonics Bases of Reading Program, First Grade, Primer Level

Step 4. Choose an observation method

There are three types of instruments that may be useful for observation depending on the circumstances of use: on-the-spot checklists, coded behavior records, delayed report instruments. Examples of these are seen in Figures 7 through 12.

On-the-spot checklists can be used for recording the presence, absence, or frequency of a few behaviors as they occur. In some circumstances, they can also be used to check the duration of an activity. They will not, however, help you to record the exact form, quality, or intensity of a particular behavior exhibited.

Two characteristics of checklists make them particularly useful instruments for small-scale evaluations, for evaluations done under time

OBSERVATION CHECKLIST

Learning Through Discovery

Make a check in the proper box each time you see the following behaviors occur during the lesson. Use one sheet for
each lesson observed. For each lesson, record the actions
of the teacher and ONE STUDENT, chosen at random.

Observer _Hellendale_   Class observed _1-C_
Date and time _Nov 20; 11Am-10:35_
Curriculum lesson number _29_ Topic _plorts??fame_
Number of students in lesson group _6_

Teacher tells the students to list the information they
have gathered so far.
᝝᝝

Teacher asks for a prediction of the results of an action (s)he is about to undertake.
//

Teacher gives class the answer to a question (s)he has
asked.
///

Teacher responds to student comment by "elaborating"
on the student's answer.
᝝᝝ //

Student writes down a comment made by the teacher, him/
herself, or another student.
᝝᝝ ᝝᝝ ᝝᝝ /

Figure 7. An on-the-spot checklist

and financial constraints, or for situations in which the evaluator is unfamiliar with program content. First, checklists count the number of times particular events occurred or particular materials or people were observed. These produce easy numbers to work with when summarizing and reporting results. Second, training observers to use a checklist is relatively easy. The evaluator needs only to ensure that the observers understand the definitions of the behaviors in question and can carry out the reporting procedure in the setting.

In general, you should consider using a checklist in these situations:

— when you can precisely define the materials, situations, activity, or event that needs to be detected and count how many times it has occurred
— when critical features of the program consist largely of materials and observables that stay put rather than activities that are more dynamic

You can use checklists for observing the occurrence of particular behaviors (for example, how many times the teacher asks a particular sort of question), but you should probably limit the number of behaviors to ten or fewer. With more than ten behaviors to look for, observers not only need to detect and classify the behaviors they witness, but they also have to find the proper place to check on the observation recording sheet. This can lead to confusion and inaccuracy. Frequency tallying means noting each occurrence of a discrete behavior. Keeping track of the frequency of certain questions in a group discussion, for example, would demand making a check on the observer's tally sheet each time the teacher asks that kind of question. Activities of some duration such as student seatwork, recess, or certain social interchanges need to be recorded differently. Measuring duration demands that you time interval samples—that is, pace observations to the passing of short time intervals, say, a few minutes. To track the duration of a group discussion, the observer would record a tally at the end of each predetermined time interval (say one minute) to show that the discussion was still underway.

Suggestions for ensuring good on-the-spot checklists:

(1) Keep the item number down, preferably below ten.
(2) Place the items in logical sequence, perhaps according to the times at which activities occur or according to the placement of materials or activity areas in the room.
(3) Make sure that observers understand your definitions of terms.
(4) Decide whether to record just occurrence or frequencies as well. If you want to know if the behavior occurred at all, single checks will be sufficient.

Which math materials were used?

____ math place-value games

____ number bingo

____ number practice cassette tapes

If you want to know how frequently an event was observed you will ask the observers to tally.

Make a check each time you see one of the following materials being used:

____ math place-value games

____ number bingo

____ number practice cassette tapes

In situations where you want to record the duration of activities, you may want to tally on a time interval sampling basis.

Example of a checklist used for monitoring activity duration. A computer-assisted instruction (CAI) program for teaching fourth-grade spelling is systematically observed for level of student participation. For two weeks an observer watches pupils working at five terminals during the daily 35-minute CAI period. The observer notes the duration of the time that each pupil actually works with the computer spelling program.

Observer _KLEIN_	Time begun _10:40 a.m._
Date _MAY 10_	Time ended _____
Class _5-D_	Number of 20-second intervals recorded _____

Time Intervals (20 seconds)

Student	Terminal	1 Y	N	2 Y	N	3 Y	N	4 Y	N	5 Y	N	6 Y	N	7 Y	N	etc.
SCHWARTZ	A	✓		✓				✓	✓							
SMITH	B	✓			✓											
GARCIA	C	✓		✓		✓		✓								
WONG	D		✓	✓			✓	✓								
O'HARA	E	✓		✓		✓			✓							
JOHNSON	B					✓		✓								
etc.																

Figure 8. Observation checklist for recording duration of time students spend at CAI terminal

Armed with a stopwatch and the checklist in Figure 8, the observer checks each pupil's behavior at the passing of 20-second intervals. If the pupil is working on the program, a check is made in the *yes* column for that interval; if the pupil is looking away or typing but not in response to program requests, then a check is made in the *no* column. The observer also notes whether a student has left the terminal altogether, placing a solid horizontal line in the remainder of that student's row. Then new students who use the terminal are entered at the bottom of the list, and the recording of on-task behavior begins again.

Figure 8 shows recording from one observer of four time intervals for six CAI students. Note that student Johnson replaced student Smith at Terminal B at the beginning of the third 20-second interval.

Example of use of an observation checklist for tallying the frequency of behaviors. The formative evaluator of the phonics program described earlier in the scenarios wishes to know whether the teachers are implementing correctly the prescribed small group lessons. The sample checklist in Figure 9 was constructed and used by observers watching randomly selected reading lessons.

Observation Checklist:
Phonics Bases of Reading

First Grade--Primer Level--Small Group Lesson

Observer_____   Class_____

Date_____   Time: From_____to_____

On the line next to each behavior, make a check each
time you see the behavior occur during the lesson.
You should use one of these lists for every lesson
observed.

Teacher presenting a phonics flashcard
asks for the sound of a letter   _____

Teacher asks for the name of a letter
on the flashcard   _____

Teacher praises a correct answer   _____

Teacher introduces a story (make one
check per sentence spoken)   _____

Teacher tells a pupil or the group to
"look at the picture"   _____

Did the lesson follow the prescribed   ☐   ☐
sequence?   yes   no

Figure 9. Observation checklist for recording
occurrence and frequency of teacher behaviors

Coded behavior records enable you to record in detail many behaviors as they occur within a given time period, but they are the most difficult observation method to use well. The technique permits you to record not only what events occurred and how many times, but also to record the sequence in which the events took place. Assignment of symbols or codes to behaviors being observed is essential to coded behavior records. The code system is then taught to observers. Here is an example of a relatively simple code system.

Basic Code:

A = teacher	r = requests	p = praises
B = helper	a = assigns	h = helps
C = child being helped		v = volunteers

Combinations of Symbols:

Arv	=	teacher requests volunteers
AaBC	=	teacher assigns one child to help another
ApB	=	teacher praises helper
ApC	=	teacher praises child being helped
BpC	=	helper praises child she is helping
Bv	=	child volunteers to help another child
Bh	=	child engages in helping behaviors
BrA	=	helper requests help from teacher
Cr	=	child requests help

Coded behavior records have two disadvantages that make them difficult data collection methods for most evaluations. First, data from coded behavior records are hard to summarize and interpret. The coded behavior record produces a string of symbols; once the observations have taken place, you must still extract data from the records. This usually entails identifying event sequences of interest and then examining the records to tally the occurrence of these sequences. Second, use of the coded behavior record requires that observers be thoroughly trained so that several observers watching the same episode produce virtually the same coded record. This means not only noticing when a target event occurs but also noting its duration and observing accurately the sequence of events in which it is embedded.

Nonetheless, coded behavior records are useful under the following circumstances:

—when you want to record the sequence in which events occurred, including sequences perhaps not prescribed
—when you want to get down in code as much as possible of what the observer sees
—when you must record many different events on the part of teachers, participants, and so on
—when the amount of time available and your own expertise make it feasible to devise the code for recording behaviors and for training observers
—when you can audio or videotape the events to be recorded so that the observer can check and recheck his coding

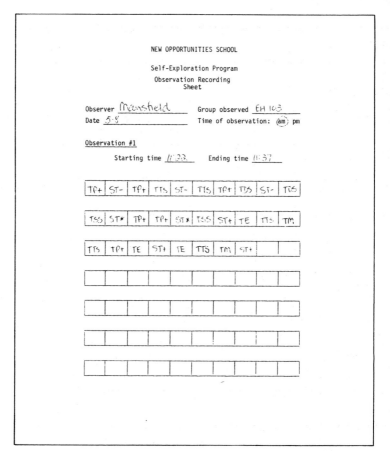

NEW OPPORTUNITIES SCHOOL

Self-Exploration Program
Observation Recording
Sheet

Observer _Mansfield_   Group observed _EH 103_
Date _5-8_   Time of observation: (am) pm

Observation #1

      Starting time _11:23_   Ending time _11:37_

TP+	ST-	TP+	TTS	ST-	TTS	TP+	TTS	ST-	TTS
TSS	ST*	TP+	TP+	ST*	TSS	ST+	TE	TTS	TM

TTS	TP+	TE	ST+	TE	TTS	TM	ST+		

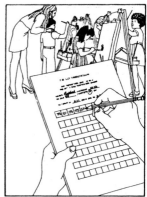

Figure 10. A coded behavior record

Coded behavior records enable you to record many different events because of the flexibility of a code system. The basic code should comprise as few symbols as possible to ensure that observers will neither forget nor confuse them.

Suggestions for effective use of coded behavior records:

(1) Devise a manageable code, one the observer can easily learn. This means that the number of symbols must be restricted; but combinations of symbols, where possible, can increase the repertoire of possible behavior descriptions.

(2) Modify the instrument as your needs require. For example, if you find that the people being observed are likely to engage in the same behavior for a period of time, you may want to build into the instrument a means for distinguishing between behaviors of long and short durations.

(3) Design the recording sheets with an eye toward information decoding and interpretation. If the job of transferring coded information to a summary sheet or to the computer can be done by a clerk or an aide, you will save time. Early attention to precisely how information will be analyzed and reported will prevent collecting unnecessary or uninterpretable data.

Delayed reports of one kind or another are commonly used observation tools. One characteristic that distinguishes them from the two previously discussed techniques is that they are filled in *after* an observation period has passed. While the amount of subjective interpretation required of the observer will vary, most delayed report instruments do require some inference or judgment. Delayed report instruments are essentially questionnaires asking about what the observer has seen. In addition to the development of the questionnaire, the delayed report method requires two basic procedures:

(1) Observers must be pre-informed about what they are looking for. They learn beforehand the nature of the questions on the questionnaire.

(2) The observation session should be as formalized as possible. The evaluator decides when it will occur, how long it will last, and who will be observed.

The simplest way to use a delayed report instrument is to have observers watch the program in operation for a specified period of time and then withdraw to fill out the questionnaire. A more complex method, but one which has advantages when you want to watch intensively particular events or people, is to sample time intervals.

Time interval sampling, depicted in Figure 12, is accomplished by

Example of a coded behavior record to find out how a program is evolving. An evaluator has been assigned the job of describing and evaluating a group inquiry science program in which teachers hold discussions to help students reason out hypotheses about various physical phenomena. The major directive to teachers, who have been extensively trained in methods of questioning, is to ask questions and make statements so as to prolong verbal interchanges with and among students. The program plan, therefore, specifies no particular type or length of interchange, only that teachers try as hard as possible to make these discussions lengthy. The teachers themselves have described their group discussion strategy in slightly more specific detail. They try to ask only questions that encourage students to use concepts, analysis, and evaluation. They do not ask "yes, no, or right answer" questions, and they try not to disagree outright with the student. Only students who have raised their hands are called on. Teachers try not to give their own opinions on the issues under discussion. They ignore disruptions. In all circumstances they try to keep the discussion going.

To see how well their description fits usual program practice, the evaluator has selected and trained two observers to watch randomly-sampled class discussions. The observers will keep a coded behavior record of each discussion. They will memorize and use a symbol system, excerpts of which comprise Figure 11. The two observers will keep a running account of comments and interactions during randomly selected 20-minute sessions over a two month period. From the strings of interactions recorded, the evaluator will be able to characterize the kinds of verbal interchanges that the program produces. She will be able to tell how many and what type of comments are made as well as what sorts of teacher remarks seem to facilitate or terminate discussion.

Code for Recording Observations
of Group Discussion

Symbol	Behavior
TY	Teacher asks a why question
TOO	Teacher asks a who question
TH	Teacher asks a how question
TD	Teacher makes a disagreeing comment
TP	Teacher paraphrases a student's comment
TR	Teacher reprimands a student
TT	Teacher asks a question or makes a statement that terminates the exchange
SO	Student expresses opinion

Figure 11. Excerpt from a code for producing
a record of science group discussion behaviors

OBSERVATION QUESTIONNAIRE

Peer Tutoring Project
(Reading Component)

Fill out this questionnaire after you have observed tutoring
for ten minutes. Fill out a different questionnaire for
every ten minutes of tutoring observed. You may take *two
minutes* for the questionnaire.

Classroom observed _Room 12_   Time: from _2:25_ to _2:35_
Observer _Lindsay_   Date _October 13_
Tutor-tutee observed _Campbell- Riley_

    0 = this did not occur during the time of observation
    1 = this happened once
    1+ = this happened more than once

Instructional quality

1. Tutor explains the identification of a
   word or a comprehension concept correctly.   0 (1) 1+
2. Tutor gives immediate feedback to tutee's
   answer.   (0) 1 1+
3. Tutor instructs tutee to "sound out" an
   unknown word.   0 1 (1+)
4. Tutor gives an answer without first asking
   the tutee to try and figure it out.   (0) 1 1+
5. Tutor gives tutee wrong answer or
   information.   0 1 1+
6. Tutor gives explanation that tutee does
   not appear to understand.   0 1 1+

Affect

7. Tutor becomes upset or angry at tutee.   0 1 1+
8. Tutor praises tutee.   0 1 1+

Task orientation

9. Tutor makes an off-the-subject comment
   to tutee.   0 1 1+
10. Tutor discourages tutee from talking
    off-the-topic.   0 1 1+
11. What percentage of the ten minutes was
    spent on activities not relevant to the
    reading lesson? _____

                                    GO ON TO NEXT PAGE.

Figure 12. A delayed-report observation instrument
using time interval sampling

dividing the total observation period into short intervals, minutes or perhaps only seconds long. The observer spends the initial portion of each interval observing and the latter part recording, then switches his or her attention back to observing and recording again. If different individuals or episodes are to be watched, the observer can shift the objects of observation after each time interval.

The delayed report method will be most useful under these circumstances:

—when you feel you can get better data by sampling from the scene periodically rather than recording whole episodes—for example, when you need data on many students working independently.

—when behaviors must be watched so carefully that recording would interfere. The delayed report method allows the observer to devote full attention to what is being seen.

—when there is a possibility that recording would intimidate, fascinate, or otherwise disturb the people being observed. The observer can record outside of the room.

The amount of training needed by observers using a delayed report method varies according to the complexity of the observed events and the amount of judgment you expect the observers to make about what they have seen.

Suggestions for effective use of delayed report instruments:

(1) When you write items, check the wording to see if you can reduce the level of observer inference or judgment and still obtain the information you need. Again, by eliminating words likely to be interpreted differently by different observers, you increase accuracy.

(2) When you determine the length of observation time units, keep in mind that the longer the delay between observation and recording, the less dependable the rating. You can narrow the time gap by time interval sampling. In this case, be sure to format your recording sheet to reflect division of the observation period into intervals.

(3) Before you design the final draft of the instrument, plan how you will analyze and report the results of the observation.

Example of the delayed report method. The evaluator of the phonics program described earlier in the scenarios wishes to describe the silent reading activities of students who are not taking part in group reading with the teacher. The program plan specifies that students who are working in their seats either (a) use workbooks, or (b) practice drill exercises with audio machines that present flash cards and read words for students. These activities are supervised by classroom volunteers and aides.

The evaluator hires two observers to watch the students' seatwork. Over the course of two weeks, these two observers each watch five students per day during the 10-minute seatwork period. The observers' 10 minutes are divided as follows: They each watch five students for four minutes apiece. Each four minute time interval involves a 3 ½-minute observation of one student followed by 30 seconds of recording. They then turn their attention to another student, observe for 3 ½ minutes, and record again.

Once you have decided whether to use a checklist, coded behavior record, or a delayed report instrument, you should make a final determination of what behaviors or events you intend to observe. Define them as precisely as possible, and rough out the instrument.

Step 5. Decide how long each observation time sample will need to last in order to yield good data

In formal observation, any one observer is responsible for watching one or more program participants or episodes for a specified period of time. The length of this time period will vary. In general, of course, time samples should be long enough so that observers can see events of interest. If the events to be recorded by observers go on continuously, then the length of time spent on observation can be as short as a few minutes, and time interval sampling can be used. In this case time interval sampling will give observers a chance to watch many different participants. The length of observation sessions will be further influenced by the number of observations needed. Ask yourself: How many observations will provide convincing evidence that the findings represent recurring behavior? At what point during the overall life of the program should these observations take place? What is the best time for the observation: mid-morning? afternoon? early in the week? Fridays? on payday?

Check with the program staff to find out how they schedule their daily and weekly activities. Find out when the program can be seen.

Step 6. Prepare a sampling plan for conducting observations

Guidelines for setting up a data collection sampling plan were discussed in Chapter 3, pages 49 to 54. In that chapter it was suggested that you either draw a sample of typical time periods of program operation at diverse sites or choose particular sites or cases for intensive study.

Besides choosing sites and times at which to conduct observations, you
will probably need to sample people and events to watch during the
observation as well. While observing in a classroom, for instance, it will
not be possible to watch each pupil and every event. You will have to be
selective. If the program prescribes a group activity, then the observer
simply watches the group. However, where many individuals or several
groups are participating, the decision about whom and what to observe
in order to get a fair representation of program events is more difficult.

To help you decide who should be the focus of observation, ask
yourself these questions:

— Do you need to focus on the teacher or leader? That is, does the program
  require specific behaviors from this person?
— Do you need to select some participants from the group because they are
  to be treated differently or are likely to respond to the program differently?
  Or are there some people who you or other evaluation audiences believe
  may have more difficulty than others participating in the program?
— Are you going to pre-select for observation and provide the observers with
  the names of specific people to watch, or are you going to ask the observer
  to make on-the-spot selections based on who is nearby or who is engaging
  in a particular activity?
— Will the observer stay with one participant or group for an entire
  observation period, or will the subjects of observations change during that
  period?
— Do you want the observer to make a quick check at any time of what all
  participants are doing?

In any case, you should try to observe as many participants as
possible and have the observers spend as much time at as many program
sites as possible. The more of this kind of data you collect, the more
representative will be the picture of the program you provide. What and
how much you observe will be determined by such practical considera-
tions as the number of observers you can recruit, the number of time
samples of the desired length you can fit in every day, and the tolerance
of the program staff for having observers present.

Step 7. Prepare the observers' recording sheets

While the examples of observation methods in Step 4 can help provide a
basic format for these methods, you will probably need to adapt the
format to your situation. If your observers are not experienced and
know little about the subject that the program addresses, then you will
have to train them so that they agree about what they see and use the

observation instrument uniformly. You will probably have to revise whatever instrument you develop initially—perhaps several times—to eliminate or adjust items with which observers have problems. To help diminish the time needed for ensuring the fit between observers and instrument, keep the instrument simple. A good rule of thumb is to design the instrument so that observers focus on behaviors and events rather than expressing opinions about these events. The language of the items can help with this. For example, a checklist entry could be phrased "Participant works on form five minutes without looking away or leaving seat," rather than "Participant is deeply engrossed by completing the form." A coded behavior symbol could consist of "Sr—student raises hand" rather than "Sn—student knows answer." Similarly, a questionnaire item from a delayed report instrument could ask

Approximately how many clients signed into the career resource area during the observations period?

___ 0-2   ___ 3-5   ___ 6-8   ___ 9-11

rather than

How interested did clients appear to be in the career resource area?

___ Very   ___ Moderately   ___ Neutral   ___ Indifferent   ___ Hostile

When looking at some program characteristics, of course, you may want observers to make inferences beyond what they see. Some complex events cannot be captured simply by counting the frequency of a particular behavior. Such is the case with the two items below, both of which require a high level of inference:

How would you rate the noise level in the classroom?

____ High (adults could not be heard)
____ Fairly high
____ Moderate
____ Fairly quiet
____ Extremely quiet

What percentage of the observation interval would you say the participants spent attending to the task at hand?

____ 80-100%
____ 60-79%
____ 40-59%
____ 20-39%
____ less than 20%

In general, the more inference you allow observers, the richer the portrait you will receive of the program; but you will have to invest much time and effort in amplifying and defining the items and training observers so that their inferences will reflect a common viewpoint.

Step 8. Choose observers

In the interest of reliability and credibility, try to use at least two observers. If you need to make a strong case for objectivity, the observers should be detached from the program and should stand neither to profit nor suffer as a result of the evaluation. Observers can generally be recruited on a volunteer or minimum salary basis from high schools or local colleges, from other schools in the district, and, in the case of a fairly large organization, from other departments.

In the case of less formal implementation evaluations you may be able to relax the rules about observer objectivity. In some cases, for example, in an exclusively formative evaluation, it may be useful to have people who planned the program or who are implementing it at another site serve as classroom observers. They may see things that the detached observer would not see or even expect to look for. Their participation as observers may push them to take a good hard look at the program or the progress it is making toward achieving its intended goals.

Step 9. Train observers and try out the instrument

Explain to your observers what you mean by formal observation and describe the behaviors they will be watching; train observers in the definitions you will be using to describe the behaviors and events that should be taking place and the materials they should see. If you are using a coded behavior record, train observers to use the code. Make flash cards and hold drills if you have to, and test observers for mastery of the definitions and code. Distribute copies of your instrument and explain how to use it. If it will not bias the results of the observation, explain to the observers why you need the information and how it will be used.

Have the observers practice. If you intend to use time interval sampling in which the observer must rapidly rotate between observing and recording, give observers stopwatches or timers and have them practice observing and recording quickly. Role-playing, watching videotapes, and practice observations in non-program classrooms are all techniques for preparing observers. Have the observers monitor each other and suggest changes in the category codings or behavior classification if they find your instructions unclear. If necessary, make changes or deletions.

Observation instruments—in fact, any measures that rely on some-one's judgment—have chronic credibility problems that are related to the issue of reliability. With these data collection methods the instru-ment, to a large extent, is a person; and the perceptions of this person may fluctuate. For example, during a Monday observation, an observer might see a teacher pick up a student's worksheet and say, "Robert! Have you done so much already?" The observer might interpret this particular behavior as asking a question. On Tuesday the same rater might observe the same behavior and interpret it as making a statement of praise. With observations, the best way to demonstrate that your evaluation has been minimally contaminated by inconsistency from "human instruments" is to use more than one observer. If different people report behavior or activities in essentially the same way, then you have evidence that the rules for recording have been well learned and uniformly applied.

If you are using interviews, you should conduct tryouts to verify that different interviewers questioning the same person will come up with the same answers.

If your instrument is an observation measure and you will be using only a single reporter, you can estimate this observer's reliability in the following way:

— First, videotape or film part of an episode which the observer will be coding.
— Then, train another person, who will act as a reliability check, to observe in the same way as your observer. Have this person watch and code the film or videotape. The reliability which you are able to calculate by correlating these two observations will give you an idea of the consistency with which your one observer can be counted on to record accurately the information obtained.

Incidentally, if you will be able to have more than one rater observe each event during actual data collection, it is good practice to include in your evaluation report the mean results calculated across raters. Because this information comes from more than one source, it will be more reliable than separate reports. If you do use more than one rater, you should consult with a data analyst to determine how to calculate.

Step 10. Inform the program staff about the upcoming observations

To let the staff know about what you intend to do, you can approach people individually, conduct a group meeting, or circulate a memo through the office of the project director or the chief administrator. Be sure to show in some way that a person in authority sanctions the observations.

You may want to introduce the observers to the program staff before they observe. No matter how you decide to introduce the observations, explain why the observers will be present and how long they will stay in one room. It is probably not a good idea to tell the staff the exact day or time when the observers will appear. Not knowing when to expect observers will discourage staff from preparing something for the observer that is not typical of the program.

Step 11. Conduct observations

Make sure the observers carry out the observations as planned. Keep careful track of problems and inconsistencies between raters so that all errors, discrepancies, or unexpected problems can be corrected before the next round of observations or can be reported in the implementation section of the report.

Step 12. When the observation data are in, score them and prepare them for interpretation and presentation

If your observation system has used either a checklist or questionnaire for recording, you will have to transfer these data from individual instruments to a data summary sheet or to a computer format, as described in Chapter 7.

If you have used a coded behavior record, then you need to further reduce the data by tallying the occurrence of symbols and symbol sequences that are of interest to you. This can be done as follows:

(1) Look over the coded sheets and decide which symbols and which symbol sequences you want to report. This may require some careful thought and extensive examination of patterns in the data. Always keep in mind what it is you expect to describe in the report.

(2) Construct a tally sheet and tally the number of occurrences of each symbol or sequence per observation or time interval.

(3) Calculate the mean number of occurrences of each symbol per group or observation that are of interest to you, for example, those from the same class or taken at the same time over the span of the program. You might also graph the distribution of the symbols, explaining the number of times each occurred per time period observed.

An Observation System You Might
Adapt to Your Own Purposes:
The Stallings Observation System

As part of an evaluation of the federal Follow-Through Program, Jane Stallings and David Kaskowitz of Stanford Research Institute (SRI) developed a method for measuring program implementation through observation. The observation instrument is available for measuring implementation of classroom programs.[1] Stallings describes the rationale for developing the system in the following way:

> Observation was the only way to see whether or not the Follow-Through Programs were successful in getting their ideas into the classroom. We [the SRI staff] had to see if the materials specified in each program were being used; if children were grouped with classroom aides and teachers as specified; and if the verbal interactions of teachers and children were those specified by the sponsor of the models. (Stallings & Kaskowitz, 1974: 25).

To meet these needs the SRI researchers developed an observation system containing three instruments:

A physical environment information form. With this, the observer describes equipment and material.

The classroom observation procedure. With this, the observer describes the general type of activities of all students and adults in the room.

The 5-minute interaction. With this, the observer records the specific behaviors that constitute interactions among various program participants during a 5-minute observation period.

The physical environment information form is a checklist. The classroom observation procedure, reproduced in Figure 13, is also a checklist, but a sophisticated one on which the observer notes, per time sample, the activities of each individual, dyad of two children, small group, and large group in the room. The possible activities (e.g., arts and crafts, games, active play) are listed on the left side of the measure. The grouping of the children is indicated by the four columns: One Child, Two Children, Small Groups, Large Groups. The letters T, A, V, and i repeated under each column stand for teacher, aide, volunteer, and independent child. The circled numbers in each column allow the observer to record, as in Figure 13 for instance, that two children are working together on math, unsupervised; two aides are each working with small groups of students in math; and one teacher is supervising a single small group in math. In the box at left center, the observer has

CLASSROOM OBSERVATION PROCEDURE

CLASSROOM CHECK LIST (be sure to code EVERYONE in the class)

	ONE CHILD	TWO CHILDREN	SMALL GROUPS	LARGE GROUPS
1. Snack, lunch	T ①②③ A ①②③ V ①②③ i ①②③	T ①②③ A ①②③ V ①②③ i ①②③	T ①②③④ A ①②③④ V ①②③④ i ①②③④	T ①② A ①② V ①② i ①②
2. Group time	T ①②③ A ①②③ V ①②③ i ①②③	T ①②③ A ①②③ V ①②③ i ①②③	T ①②③④ A ①②③④ V ①②③④ i ①②③④	T ①② A ①② V ①② i ①②
Story 3. Music Dancing	T ①②③ A ①②③ V ①②③ i ①②③	T ①②③ A ①②③ V ①②③ i ①②③	T ①②③④ A ①②③④ V ①②③④ i ①②③④	T ①② A ①② V ①② i ①②
4. Arts, Crafts	T ①②③ A ①②③ V ①②③ i ①②③	T ①②③ A ①②③ V ①②③ i ①②③	T ①②③④ A ①②③④ V ①②③④ i ①②③④	T ①② A ①② V ①② i ①②
Guessing Games 5. Table Games Puzzles	T ①②③ A ①②③ V ①②③ i ①②③	T ①②③ A ①②③ V ①②③ i ①②③	T ①②③④ A ①②③④ V ①②③④ i ①②③④	T ①② A ①② V ①② i ①②
6. Math — Numbers / Arithmetic	T ①②③ A ①②③ V ①②③ i ●②③	T ①②③ A ①②③ V ①②③ i ●②③	T ●②③④ A ①●③④ V ①②③④ i ①②③④	T ①② A ①② V ①② i ①②
7. Reading / Alphabet / Lang Development	T ①②③ A ①②③ V ①②③ i ①②③	T ①②③ A ①②③ V ①②③ i ①②③	T ①②③④ A ①②③④ V ①②③④ i ①②③④	T ①② A ①② V ①② i ①②
8. Social Studies / Geography	T ①②③ A ①②③ V ①②③ i ①②③	T ①②③ A ①②③ V ①②③ i ①②③	T ①②③④ A ①②③④ V ①②③④ i ①②③④	T ①② A ①② V ①② i ①②
9. Science / Natural World	T ①②③ A ①②③ V ①②③ i ①②③	T ①②③ A ①②③ V ①②③ i ①②③	T ①②③④ A ①②③④ V ①②③④ i ①②③④	T ①② A ①② V ①② i ①②
10. Sewing / Cooking / Pounding / Sawing	T ①②③ A ①②③ V ①②③ i ①②③	T ①②③ A ①②③ V ①②③ i ①②③	T ①②③④ A ①②③④ V ①②③④ i ①②③④	T ①② A ①② V ①② i ①②
11. Blocks / Trucks	T ①②③ A ①②③ V ①②③ i ①②③	T ①②③ A ①②③ V ①②③ i ①②③	T ①②③④ A ①②③④ V ①②③④ i ①②③④	T ①② A ①② V ①② i ①②
12. Dramatic Play / Dress-Up	T ①②③ A ①②③ V ①②③ i ①②③	T ①②③ A ①②③ V ①②③ i ①②③	T ①②③④ A ①②③④ V ①②③④ i ①②③④	T ①② A ①② V ①② i ①②
13. Active Play	T ①②③ A ①②③ V ①②③ i ①②③	T ①②③ A ①②③ V ①②③ i ①②③	T ①②③④ A ①②③④ V ①②③④ i ①②③④	T ①② A ①② V ①② i ①②
14. RELIABILITY SHEET ○				

Left-side material key (adjacent to rows 6–9):

○ TV
○ Audio-Visual Materials
○ Exploratory Materials
○ Math and Science Equipment
● Texts, Workbooks
● Puzzles, Games

Figure 13. Classroom observation procedure

	ONE CHILD	TWO CHILDREN	SMALL GROUPS	LARGE GROUPS
15. Practical Skills Acquisition	T ①②③ A ①②③ V ①②③ I ①②③	T ①②③ A ①②③ V ①②③ I ①②③	T ①②③④ A ①②③④ V ①②③④ I ①②③④	T ①② A ①② V ①② I ①②
16. Observing	T ①②③ A ①②③ V ①②③ I ①②③	T ①②③ A ①②③ V ①②③ I ①②③	T ①②③④ A ①②③④ V ①②③④ I ①②③④	T ①② A ①② V ①② I ①②
17. Social Interaction Ob [ⓒ ② ⓢ]	ⓣ T ①②③ ⓐ A ①②③ ⓥ V ①②③ I ①②③	T ①②③ A ①②③ V ①②③ I ①②③	T ①②③④ A ①②③④ V ①②③④ I ①②③④	T ①② A ①② V ①② I ①②
18. Unoccupied Child	T ①②③ A ①②③ V ①②③ I ①②③	T ①②③ A ①②③ V ①②③ I ①②③	T ①②③④ A ①②③④ V ①②③④ I ①②③④	T ①② A ①② V ①② I ①②
19. Discipline	T ①②③ A ①②③ V ①②③ I ①②③	T ①②③ A ①②③ V ①②③ I ①②③	T ①②③④ A ①②③④ V ①②③④ I ①②③④	T ①② A ①② V ①② I ①②
20. Transitional Activities	ⓣ T ①②③ ⓐ A ①②③ ⓥ V ①②③ I ①②③	T ①②③ A ①②③ V ①②③ I ①②③	T ①②③④ A ①②③④ V ①②③④ I ①②③④	T ①② A ①② V ①② I ①②
21. Classroom Management	ⓣ T ①②③ ⓐ A ①②③ ⓥ V ①②③ I ①②③	T ①②③ A ①②③ V ①②③ I ①②③	T ①②③④ A ①②③④ V ①②③④ I ①②③④	T ①② A ①② V ①② I ①②
22. Out of Room	ⓣ T ①②③ ⓐ A ①②③ ⓥ V ①②③ I ①②③	T ①②③ A ①②③ V ①②③ I ①②③	T ①②③④ A ①②③④ V ①②③④ I ①②③④	T ①② A ①② V ①② I ①②

NUMBER OF ADULTS IN CLASSROOM   ⓪ ① ② ● ④ ⑤ ⑥ ⑦ ⑧ ⑨ ⑩

Figure 13 Continued

indicated that materials in use by the dyad and small groups are texts, workbooks, puzzles and games. Stallings has adapted the classroom observation procedure for use in classrooms from a broad range of educational programs: group process, developmental, exploratory, cognitive, programmed instruction, and fundamental school classroom models.

The third part of the Stallings observation procedure, the 5-minute interaction shown in Figure 14, records interpersonal exchanges among teachers, students, aides, and others in the classroom. The system categorizes behavioral and verbal interchanges and records their emotional tone (happy, unhappy). The instrument resembles a coded behavior record, and so the observer needs to memorize a fairly complex code. Rather than write down the codes from memory, however, the observer darkens cells on a computer scorable form. The Stallings system comes complete with flash cards to help observers learn the code.

List of Codes

Who/To Whom	What	How
T — Teacher	1 — Command or Request	H — Happy
A — Aide	2 — Open-ended Question	U — Unhappy
V — Volunteer	3 — Response	N — Negative
C — Child	4 — Instruction,	T — Touch
D — Different Child	Explanation	Q — Question
2 — Two Children	5 — Comments, Greetings;	G — Guide/Reason
S — Small Group (3-8)	General Action	P — Punish
L — Large Group (9 up)	6 — Task-related Statement	O — Object
An — Animal	7 — Acknowledge	W — Worth
M — Machine	8 — Praise	DP — Dramatic
	9 — Corrective Feedback	Play/Pretend
	10 — No Response	A — Academic
	11 — Waiting	B — Behavior
	12 — Observing, Listening	
	NV — Nonverbal	
	X — Movement	

R — Repeat the frame
S — Simultaneous action
C — Cancel the frame

Figure 14. List of codes for the "5-minute interaction"
in the Stallings observation system

Because of its already considerable use, the care with which it was developed, and its potential applicability, the Stallings observation method is recommended for assessing the implementation of programs where the classroom is the unit of study.

Note

1. The observation system as first developed is described in Stallings and Kaskowitz (1974). The system that is more broadly available, complete with suggestions of its modification for use in various classrooms, is contained in Stallings (1977).

For Further Reading

Good, T. L., & Brophy, J. E. (1984). *Looking in classrooms* (3rd ed.). New York: Harper & Row.

Stallings, J. A. (1985). *Stallings' observation instrument: Training manual.* Nashville, TN: Vanderbilt University, Peabody Center for Effective Teaching.

Chapter 7
Summarizing, Analyzing, and Reporting Your Data

This chapter is intended to help you consolidate and present the data you have collected, regardless of your evaluation's purpose, methodology, or intended outcomes. As discussed in Chapter 1, there are at least four general outcomes of an implementation study. The first and often major one is, of course, to demonstrate program accountability. A second is to describe the program and perhaps to comment about how well it matches what was intended. A third outcome is to examine relationships between program characteristics and outcomes or relationships among different aspects of the program's implementation. Examining relationships means exploring—often statistically—the hypothesis on which the program is based, answering such questions as these: Do smaller classes achieve more? Are quality circles related to product quality and staff morale? Do new hires respond more favorably to off-site training than do career people? The fourth and final outcome of an implementation study is to help program staff improve the program's functioning. In each of these cases, careful analysis of data will enable you to reduce uncertainties about what has happened in the program and report your findings to the relevant audiences.

The chapter has four sections:

—a description of the use of data summary sheets for collecting item-by-item results from questionnaires, interviews, or observation sheets
—directions for reducing a large number of narrative documents (such as diaries or responses to open-ended questionnaires or interviews) to a shorter but representative narrative form
—directions for categorizing a large number of narrative documents so that they can be summarized in quantitative form
—an outline for reporting an implementation evaluation

Data summary and analysis is not an easy task, and the content of a short chapter is clearly insufficient to guarantee that this part of your evaluation will be appropriate and rigorous. For these reasons, issues related to quantitative data analysis are not discussed here. If your evaluation will rely heavily on the results of data analysis—and most will—it makes sense to consult books specifically devoted to such topics or to consult with a statistician who can assure you that what you are doing is correct.

**Preparing a Data Summary Sheet for
Scoring by Hand or by Computer**

To handle data efficiently, you should prepare a data summary sheet or computer format for each measurement instrument you use—if possible, at the time you design or select the instrument. Data summary sheets will help you interpret the data you collect and support your narrative presentation because they assist you in searching for patterns of responses that allow you to characterize the program. They also assist you in doing calculation with your data, should you need to do this.

Data summary sheets or computer-coded data require either that you have closed-response data or that open-ended responses have been categorized and coded. Closed-response data include item results from structured observation instruments, interviews, or questionnaires. These instruments produce tallies or numbers. If, on the other hand, you have item results that are narrative in form, as from open-ended questions on a questionnaire, interview, or naturalistic observation report, then you will first have to categorize and code these responses. (Suggestions for coding open-response data appear on pages 120-121.)

The first part of the following discussion deals with recording and analyzing by hand; the latter part deals with summary sheets for machine scoring and computer analysis. When scoring by hand, you can choose between two ways of summarizing the data: the quick-tally sheet and the people-time roster.

A *quick-tally* sheet displays all response options for each item so that you can tally the number of times people chose each option, as in the examples on pages 117-119. The quick-tally sheet allows you to calculate two descriptive statistics for each group whose answers are tallied: (1) the number or percentage of persons who answered each item a certain way; and (2) the average response to each item (with standard deviation) in cases where an average is a meaningful summary. Notice that with a quick-tally sheet you "lose" the individual person—that is, you no longer have access to individual response patterns. That is perfectly acceptable if all you want to know is how many or what percentage of the total group responded in a particular way. You do lose, however, the capacity to look at relationships between different responses.

If you are interested in calculating correlations, you will need to know about the response patterns of individuals within the group and probably will want to use a computer for your work. If for some reason the computer option is not possible, then you will need to create a *people-item data roster.* On such a roster, the items are listed across the top of the page. The people (classrooms, program sites, and so on) are listed in a vertical column on the left. They are usually identified by number. Graph paper or the kind of paper used for computer programming is useful for constructing these data rosters, even when the data are to be processed by hand rather than by computer. The people-item data roster showing the results recorded from the completed classroom observation response that precedes it are presented in Figure 15.

The small numerals in the response cells of the observation response form indicate points assigned to each answer for scoring. Unless necessary, they should not appear on the response form when it is used by an observer. Since the items in the above example can go in either direction—"applies to none" can be a desirable or undesirable response depending on the item wording—the most desirable response is coded "4" and the least desirable response is coded "1." Besides permitting you to calculate the same descriptive statistics as the quick-tally sheet, the people-item data roster will allow you to compute a total or average score for each person, classroom, program site, and so on.

Figure 15 shows a data roster from a classroom observation study in which three observers took part. The evaluator has chosen to record the scores in such a way as to keep the observers' responses separate from one another. The major interest, however, remains that of obtaining scores for each of the classrooms. Setting up the summary sheet in this way has the additional benefit of providing a quick check on inter-rater reliability, that is, consistency across observers.

Automated data processing, including machine scoring and analysis of your data, will either affect the format of the data summary sheet or make it unnecessary to have one at all. Since machine scoring and computer analysis packages are becoming increasingly available at offices and schools, it is possible that you can conserve your own time by

Example

Observation Instrument (from observer 1 for classroom 1)

```
Rate the quality of the group interaction you
observed using the scale provided.
              1 - unsatisfactory
              2 - poor
              3 - so-so
              4 - good
              5 - outstanding

1.  The harmony with which the working group func-
    tioned.
          1       2       3      ④      5

2.  The involvement of all members in contributing
    to group planning.
          1       2      ③       4       5

3.  The ability of the group to proceed without
    teacher assistance.
          1       2     ③       4       5
```

Summary Sheet (people-item format)

		Item 1	Item 2	Item 3	etc.
Classroom 1	Observer 1	4	3	3	
	Observer 2				
	Observer 3				
	AVERAGE				
Classroom 2	Observer 1				
	Observer 2				
	Observer 3				
	AVERAGE				

etc.

Figure 15

Example of a people-item data roster

Observation Response Form (results from classroom 1)

Implementation Objective: Students will direct and monitor their own progress in math activities. During the math period:	applies to most	applies to some	applies to a few	applies to none
1. Students worked on individual math assignments.	4	✓ 3	2	1
2. Students asked for help with finding materials to work on.	1	2	3	✓ 4
3. Students loitered about, working at no activity in particular.	1	2	3	✓ 4
4. Students used self-testing sheets.	4	✓ 3	2	1
5. Students sought out aide ~~ect~~ ~~testing~~				✓

Summary Sheet (people-item format)

	Item 1	Item 2	Item 3	Item 4	Item 5	Item 6	etc.
Classroom 1	3	4	4	3	4	4	
Classroom 2							
Classroom 3							

etc.

Examples of quick-tally sheets

Questionnaire

		uncer-		
yes	no	tain		
☐	☐	☐	1.	Were the materials available when you needed them?
☐	☐	☐	2.	Were the materials suitable for your students

Figure 15 Continued

Summary Sheet (quick-tally format)

Item #	yes	no	uncertain
1	~~||||~~ ||||	|||	||
2	|	~~||||~~ ~~||||~~ ||	|

etc.

Observation Instrument

```
Rate the quality of the group interaction you
observed using the scale provided.
                1 - unsatisfactory
                2 - poor
                3 - so-so
                4 - good
                5 - outstanding

1 2 3 4 5   1.  The harmony with which the working
                group functioned

1 2 3 4 5   2.  The involvement of all members in
                contributing to group planning.
```

Summary Sheet (quick-tally format)

Item #	1 unsatis- factory	2 poor	3 so-so	4 good	5 out- standing
1	|	|		||	~~||||~~ |
2		|||	|||	~~||||~~	

etc.

Figure 15 Continued

investigating the availability of these services. Call a statistician, the central research and evaluation office (if one exists), or local data processing companies. If you find that automated data processing fits your time and budget constraints, then your data summary sheet will need to conform to the machine's and program's requirements. You may even find that, formatted properly, your recording form can be scored directly by machine or that you can use a machine-scorable answer sheet to bypass the need for a data summary sheet. The books suggested at the end of this chapter provide additional information about computer analysis of your data. You may also wish to read *How to Use Qualitative Methods in Evaluation* (Volume 4 of the *Program Evaluation Kit*).

Summarizing Open-Ended Responses

If you have to summarize answers to open-response questionnaire items, diary or journal entries, unstructured interviews, observations, or narrative reports of any sort, you will want a systematic way to proceed. The number of computer programs for helping analyze open-ended data grows daily, and you would do well to check on the availability and appropriateness of one for your purpose. However, the following list, adapted to your own needs, should help you to design your own system for analysis if need be. What you will eventually end up with is a set of information categories or classes that describe your data plus the frequency with which each category is mentioned.

(1) Begin by writing a unique identification number on each separate source of data (e.g., each questionnaire, each journal). If used properly, these numbers will enable you to return to the original document if you need to check exact wording.

(2) If you have sufficient time, read quickly through the materials you are trying to summarize, looking for major themes, categories, and issues, as well as critical incidents and particularly expressive quotations. Mark all of these.

(3) Set up a recording system. If you are analyzing the data by hand, obtain several sheets of plain paper to use as tally sheets. Divide each paper into four cells by drawing lines:

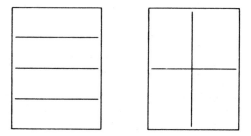

If you have access to a microcomputer and can type quickly and accurately, consider typing the data in instead of using paper to avoid having to copy data by hand.

(4) Start summarizing. Select one of the reports, and look for the kinds of events, situations, or reactions it describes or, if you completed step 2, for

evidence of the major categories you have already determined. As soon as an event is described, write a short summary of it in a cell on one of the tally sheets. You may also wish to copy an exact quotation if it is particularly well worded. *Be sure to include the identification number of the report in parentheses following the summary* so that if you need to return to the original you will not have to go through all of the documents to find it. Then, in one corner of the cell, tally a "1" to indicate that that statement has been made in one report.

If you come upon a previously unmentioned idea (event, situation, or reaction) as you read the rest of the response, summarize it in a cell and give it a singly tally for having appeared once. When you have read through the entire response, put a check or other mark on it to indicate that you have attended to it. If you are summarizing open-ended questionnaire results and have 30 or fewer respondents, you may want to copy the responses to each item in order to put in one place the specific answers to a given question. You will probably find it easiest to attend to one item or category at a time.

(5) Read the rest of the reports in any order. Record new occurrences as above. When you come upon one that seems to have been mentioned in a previous response, find the cell that summarizes it. Read carefully, making sure that both responses are really similar. Record another "1" in the cell to show that it has been mentioned in another response. In addition, if some part of the response differs substantially from or adds a significant element to the first, also write a statement that covers this different aspect in a new cell so that you may tally the number of instances in which this new element appears.

(6) Tally the references to each type of response and prepare summaries of the most frequent statements for inclusion in your report.

You will want to record and summarize data from different groups separately if the reporters faced circumstances that would predictably bring about different results (e.g., different grade levels, different program variations or sites) or if their backgrounds or positions might cause them to have different perceptions. Also, if the quantity of the data that you are gleaning from the reports appears to be unwieldy or lacking specific focus, you may need to reorganize your category system—in some cases making categories more general, in others more narrow. Whenever you form a new category system, however, heed this caution: Do not try to transfer previous tallies from the original categories to your new category system. The only safe procedure is to return to the original source, the reports themselves, and then tally results for the new categories.

How to Summarize a Large Number of
Narrative Reports by Categorizing

The following procedure helps you to assign numerical values to different types of responses and use these data in further statistical analyses. Suppose, for example, you asked 100 employees to describe their experiences at a staff development center where they received training in word processing techniques. After reading their reports and summarizing them in paragraph form, you wonder how closely the practices of the center conform to the official description of the instruction it offers. You can summarize your results by categorizing respondents' reports into, say, five degrees of closeness to official staff development center descriptions—very close, through so-so, to downright contradictory—giving each person's response a rating 1 through 5. Such rank-order data will give you a quantitative summary of people's experiences of the program. Perhaps you can then correlate this with their liking for the program or their productivity on the job.

The difficulty of the task of categorizing open-response data will vary from one situation to another. Precise instructions for arriving at categories and summarizing data cannot be provided, but the following advice should help make the task more manageable:

(1) Think of a dimension along which program implementation may vary— for example, closeness of fit to the program plan, approximation to a theory, or effectiveness of instruction. The dimension you choose should characterize the kinds of reports given to you so that you can put them in order from desirable to undesirable.

(2) Read what you consider to be a representative sampling of the data (about 25%). Determine if it is possible to begin with three general categories: (a) clearly desirable, (b) clearly undesirable, and (c) those in between.

(3) If the data can be divided in these three piles, you can then put aside for the moment those in categories a and b and proceed to refine category c by dividing it into three piles:

— those that are more desirable than undesirable
— those that are more undesirable than desirable
— those in between

(4) Refine categories a and b as you did c. If you cannot divide them into three gradations along the dimension you have chosen, then use two; or if the initial breakdown seems as far as you can go, leave it as is.

(5) Have one or more people check your categories. This can be done by asking others to go through a similar categorization process or to critique

the categories and the selections you have made. Once you have assigned numbers to your narrative data, you can proceed with statistical analyses. How meaningful such analyses will be depends on the quality of your categorization; the procedures should be done carefully and checked thoroughly.

An Outline for an Implementation Report

At last you have finished collecting and analyzing data and are ready to report what you have learned to the appropriate decision makers. Research on evaluation use suggests that useful reports take a variety of forms, from casual conversations over coffee, to working meetings, to formal documents typed and bound. An effective evaluator will report information about program implementation regularly and in a variety of ways. In all likelihood you have already started the reporting process, providing bits and pieces of information as they have emerged. Few evaluators keep good—or bad—news secret, springing it on key people at the end of the evaluation process. Such ongoing reporting is often informal, but most implementation evaluations, whether formative or summative, eventually result in a formal report of one sort or another.

For a general discussion on the preparation of evaluation reports, you should refer to *How to Communicate Evaluation Findings* (Volume 9 of the *Program Evaluation Kit*). Whether or not you become embroiled in reporting means and percentages, you will certainly want to use the data you collect to underpin some sort of program description. Such descriptions range from the very simple to the highly complicated, from narrative accounts or descriptive tables such as Table 2 or Table 8, to detailed formal reports, printed and bound. The form of report you choose should match the purpose of your evaluation. Table 8 best suits interim formative reports concerned with how faithfully the program's schedule of implementation conforms to the original plan. A formative evaluator can use this table to report, for instance, the results of monthly site visits to both the program director and the staff at different locations. Each brief interim report consists of a table, plus accompanying comments explaining why you have assigned ratings of "U," unsatisfactory implementation.

A formal implementation evaluation report typically has major parts: summary; context; the evaluation process; critical program features; results and discussions; and conclusions. The outline that follows will produce a report that describes program implementation *only*. In most evaluations, implementation issues constitute only one

TABLE 8

Project Monitoring

Objective 6: By February 29, 19YY, each participating school will implement, evaluate results, and make revisions in a program for the establishment of a positive climate for learning.

Winona School District
Wiley School

Activities for this objective	19XX				19YY					
	Sep	Oct	Nov	Dec	Jan	Feb	Mar	Apr	May	Jun
6.1 Identify staff to participate		I	C							
6.2 Selected staff members review ideas, goals, and objectives		I	P	P	C					
6.3 Identify student needs		U	I	P	C					
6.4 Identify parent needs		U	I	P	C					
6.5 Identify staff needs		U	I	P	C					
6.6 Evaluate data collected in 6.3 – 6.5						I	U	C		
6.7 Identify and prioritize specific outcome goals and objectives			I	U	P	P	C			
6.8 Identify existing policies, procedures, and laws dealing with positive school climate		U	I	P	P	C				

Evaluator's Periodic Progress Rating:
I = Activity Initiated   P = Satisfactory Progress
C = Activity Completed   U = Unsatisfactory Progress

SOURCE: This table has been adapted from a formative monitoring procedure developed by Marvin C. Alkin.

facet of a more elaborate enterprise concerned with both implementation and the actual outcomes of the program. If your evaluation focus extends beyond mere implementation, then you will need to incorporate information from the outline here into a larger report discussing other aspects of the program and its evaluation. If, in fact, the evaluation compares the effects of two different programs considered equally important by your audience, then you should prepare an implementation report that describes them both and discusses their relative outcomes.

(1) *Summary*. The summary is a brief overview of the report, explaining *why* a description of implementation has been undertaken and listing the major conclusions and recommendations to be found in the final section of the full report. Since the summary is designed for people who are too busy to read the entire report—and that may include

a large percentage of your audience—it should be limited to one or two pages maximum. Although the summary is placed *first* in the report, it is the *last* section to be written.

(2) *Context.* The second section of the report contains a description of the setting in which the program has been implemented, focusing mainly on the administrative arrangements, personnel, and resources involved.

This section sets the program in context. It describes how the program was initiated, what it was supposed to do, and the resources available. The amount of information presented will depend on the audiences for whom the report has been prepared. If the audience has no knowledge of the program, the program must be fully described. If, on the other hand, the implementation report is mainly intended for internal use and its readers are likely to be familiar with the program, this section can be brief and set down information "for the record." Regardless of the audience, if your report will be written, it might become the only lasting record of the program's implementation. In this case, the context section should contain considerable data.

If your program's setting includes many different sites or schools, it may not be practical to cover every evaluation issue separately for each. Instead, for each issue indicate similarities and differences among schools or sites or the range represented or the most typical pattern that occurred.

(3) *Program goals and characteristics.* The third section of your report should describe the program's intentions as you have come to know them from reading program materials, talking with staff, observing activities, and collecting data. While the context section describes the program's setting, this section paints a picture of the program itself so that outsiders and insiders alike will understand exactly what it is that your report will discuss. Please note that this section is appropriate both for evaluations following a quantitative approach and those using qualitative methods. This description boils down essentially to an outline of the major materials to be used, the activities engaged in, the person responsible for implementing each program feature, and the target participants in each activity. It might also include a projection of the amount of progress expected in each activity by a certain time.

If your evaluation is comparing the program with a *control,* the program received by control groups will need to be described as well, and in as much detail as possible. The extent of this description will depend on your audience's intentions regarding the control group's program. If the program is a viable alternative for adoption in lieu of or in addition to the program under scrutiny, then the description of the implementation of the control program should be as extensively and carefully treated as the description of the program under scrutiny. If the control program is *not* in contention for possible adoption, then you will need to describe only those aspects of the control program that might most strongly affect the outcomes of that program. If the control students received *no* program aimed at objectives similar to the program being studied, then you should still include a description of what the control students did while the program students were engaged in program activities.

(4) *The evaluation process.* This section includes a description of the implementation evaluation itself—the choice of measures, the range of program activities examined, the sites studied, and so forth. This section also includes a rationale for choosing the data sources listed.

(5) *Discussion* of program implementation, including the results and interpretations of implementation measures. To the extent that statistical tables communicate the evaluation results meaningfully, they should be included here, but always with explanations that a layperson can understand. Relying on available data, this section of the report can do one of two things:

(a) where appropriate, describe the extent to which the program as implemented fit the one that was planned or prescribed by a plan, theory, or teaching model

(b) describe implementation independent of underlying intent. This description, usually gathered using qualitative methods, reflects a decision that the evaluator describe what was discovered rather than comparing program events with underlying points of view.

In either case, this section describes what has been found, noting variations in the program across sites or time.

(6) *Conclusions, commendations, and recommendations.* If people read only one section of your report, this is the section they are likely to flip to. Here at last are the outcomes of all the evaluation activity that has preceded, outcomes that program staff may consider the bottom line of their efforts. This is the reason to include both commendations—praising what is right about the program—*and* recommendations for program change and development. In cases where recommendations are

likely to be controversial, they should be thoroughly supported by backup data.

Summary

This final chapter has addressed some of the issues you will face after you have collected your implementation data. Specifically it has discussed how to prepare data summary sheets, how to reduce narrative documents to usable form (whether narrative or quantitative), and how to organize an implementation report. Because the quality of your analysis and reporting may well determine the extent to which your evaluation is used by appropriate decision makers, you may choose to refer to the additional sources listed at the end of this chapter. In any event, once your data are analyzed and your report is written, your evaluation will be completed and you will, we trust, be able to congratulate yourself on a job well done.

For Further Reading

Boruch, R., & Rindskopf, D. (1984). Data analysis. In L. Rutman (Ed.), *Evaluation research methods* (pp. 121-158). Newbury Park, CA: Sage.

Fitz-Gibbon, C. T., & Morris, L. L. (1987). *How to analyze data.* Newbury Park, CA: Sage.

Fowler, F. J. (1984). *Survey research methods.* Newbury Park, CA: Sage.

Gay, L. R. (1987). *Educational research, competencies for analysis and application* (3rd ed.). Columbus, OH: Merrill.

Gray, P. J. (1984). Microcomputers in evaluation. *Evaluation News, 1-5.*

Madron, T. W., Tate, C. N., & Brookshire, R. G. (1985). Using microcomputers in research. *Qualitative applications in the social sciences* (Vol. 52). Newbury Park, CA: Sage.

Morris, L. L.,. Fitz-Gibbon, C. T., & Freeman, M. (1987). *How to communicate evaluation findings..* Newbury Park, CA: Sage.

References

Borich, G. D., & Madden, S. K. (1977). *Evaluating classroom instruction: A sourcebook of instruments.* Reading, MA: Addison-Wesley.

Buros, O. (Ed.). *Mental measurement yearbooks* (all).

Evertson, C. M., & Green, J. L. (1986). Observation as inquiry and method. In M. C. (Ed.), *Handbook of research on teaching* (3rd ed.). New York: Macmillan.

Guba, E. G., & Lincoln, Y. S. (1981). *Effective evaluation.* San Francisco: Jossey-Bass.

Journal of Classroom Interaction. (19XX). *21*(2).

Joyce, B., & Weil, M. (1983). *Models of teaching* (2nd ed.). Englewood Cliffs, NJ: Prentice-Hall.

Patton, M. Q. (1987). *How to use qualitative methods in evaluation.* Newbury Park, CA: Sage.

Simon, A., & Boyer, E. G. (1974). *Mirrors for behavior: An anthology of classroom observation instruments.* Philadelphia: Research for Better Schools, Center for the Study of Teaching.

Stallings, J. A. (1977). *Learning to look: A handbook on classroom observation and teaching models.* Belmont, CA: Wadsworth.

Stallings, J. A., & Kaskowitz, D. (1974). *Follow-through classroom observation 1972-1973.* Menlo Park, CA: Stanford Research Institute.

Appendix:
Questions for an
Implementation Evaluation

While the following list includes over 300 questions, any claim to inclusiveness is at least partly facetious; every program has unique features that will generate questions of a highly individual nature. But at the same time, the list of questions that follows, generated from the experience of many evaluators with many programs, may enable you to focus on aspects of the program you might not otherwise have seen as important. You may find it helpful to think of this list as an outline for what you will report to individuals who will use the results of your evaluation. The headings and questions are organized according to what could eventually become sections of a formal implementation report.

In organizing your evaluation, you will need to decide on two things: (1) *what* to describe about the program; and (2) what portions of your description must be supported by *corroborating evidence*. The necessity to collect supporting data to underlie your description of program features will, of course, be primarily a function of the setting of *your* evaluation. But there are program features that, because of their complexity, controversial nature, or critical weight within programs, usually require backup data regardless of the context. To remind you that your description of certain features may be met with skepticism, an asterisk appears next to questions whose answers may require accompanying evidence.

General Questions About the Program

A. Program Context

Where exactly has the program been implemented? What are these communities and locales like in general? From what states, regions, communities, or neighborhoods have program participants come?

How many and what sorts of people does the program affect? What are the characteristics of the population affected (e.g., its density, ethnic grouping, mobility rate, birth and divorce rates, percentage of young and aged)?*

What are the economic characteristics of the setting? What are the major occupations of people in the locale? What is the unemployment rate or trend?* What proportion of families are receiving welfare assistance?*

What special interest groups affect events in the locale? Is there an individual or a segment of the community that is particularly powerful or has strongly influenced the program?

What are the major characteristics of the program site or the state, district, or location in which the program took place? What clientele or grade levels are served? How many pupils or employees are in the system? How many schools, classrooms, or sites are there? What type? What is the average pupil-teacher or participant-instructor ratio? Are there any significant trends in school system or program enrollments, attendance, withdrawals, or transfers?*

What does (do) the program site(s) actually look like? What are the physical surroundings and materials? What are the key actors in program activities like? How do they feel about the program? Why did they become involved?

What is the financial status of the school system or the program's sponsor? What is the system's financial history? What is the per pupil cost of education?*

What accountability issues affect the program? Are there certain areas for which dollar amounts must be spent and for which the program is accountable? Are there program elements that staff *must* implement, such as delivery of particular program services to children in an area of special education?

B. Program Origins and History

Did the program exist prior to the time period covered in the present report? Was it known by the same title as the present program? What evidence of previous success or failure is available?*

How did the program get started? Who was instrumental in getting the program off the ground? What were their motivations and intentions? Whose idea was it to implement this particular version of the program? How did the idea develop to the point of a complete program? Who motivated the program development? Who designed, developed, or chose it? By what authority?

If the program is a modification of a previously existing program, have the characteristics of the participants changed? Have the characteristics of the program changed? If so, why?

What problems, if any, were encountered in gaining acceptance of the program by staff, administration, parents, or the community? How were these solved?

Was a formal or informal *needs assessment* conducted prior to beginning the program?[1] If so, who conducted the needs assessment, and what was its starting point? If not, how were needs determined?

Who determined the needs: Program staff? A committee of local citizens? Central administrators? Prominent or vocal individuals or groups? Who were they? Why did they become involved?

How were the needs of students or participants identified? Through a survey?* Through standardized testing?* Through recognition of disturbing events (e.g., a high dropout rate, delinquency, illiteracy, a rising crime rate, poor school attendance or on-the-job performance)? Through training needs established by employers or college admissions requirements?

Were the opinions of top management, "experts," parents, teachers, counselors, community, or potential participants solicited? What were these opinions?*

What *specific* needs guided program development? What priorities were determined? By whom and how?* How were these needs translated into goals or objectives for the program?

C. Program Rationale, Goals, and Objectives

Is there a written rationale for the program? That is, why do the program's planners feel that the various program materials and activities they have selected will lead to the achievement of program goals? If there is no explicit rationale, what is the implicit rationale behind the program? Are staff and participants aware of the rationale?

What generally was the program designed to accomplish? What underlying educational goals were set? How were they set, and by whom?*

Is there a set of written objectives for the program? If not, what are the program's objectives? How were they selected, and by whom?

Did program staff use the established needs or priorities as a basis for developing objectives? Did staff select objectives from other programs or from available collections to meet the established priorities? Are there obvious omissions?

What was the review process for the objectives before their inclusion in the program? Are the objectives realistic?

Do the objectives focus on program activities (what the program will do), on intended outcomes (what participants will learn), or on both?

Are specific evaluation activities explicit or implicit in the objectives? What are they?

D. Program Personnel

What kinds and numbers of staff took part in the program?* How can their roles be best described: Instructional versus non-instructional? Administrative, instructional, or support staff? Is an organizational chart available? Are written job descriptions available? Do they accurately reflect what people did?

Are staff members required to have special backgrounds or credentials? Do they?* What procedures were used for selecting the staff? Were any positions difficult to fill? Why? What procedures were used for training the staff?* Was the training adequate?

What special problems have been addressed in developing and maintaining staff morale? How much staff turnover has there been? For what reason?

How much time do people in each staff role devote to responsibilities connected with the program?

As the program has evolved, have certain job roles dropped out? Were some roles changed or others added? Why? How has this affected the program's functioning?

How do parents or other outside individuals participate in the program? Are they actively involved in the classroom? Do they work as advisors, counselors, mentors, instructors? How many and which parents have participated?* If parents serve as advisors, what percentage of parents actually advise? Are these parents typical of the school-parent group as a whole?*

Is parental permission required for students to participate in program activities? Has it been obtained?* How?*

E. Program Participants

For what participants was the program designed (age, grade level, ability, previous experience)? Is the program serving the individuals it is meant to?* If not, why not?

How many participants have been served by the particular program during the evaluation? What identification and recruitment efforts have program staff made?

On what basis have participants (students, classrooms, schools, districts) been selected for the program?* For example, were students with high need in the particular content area assigned to the program? If so, how was high need determined? How does the selection process work? Are participants to remain in the program for its duration? If not, what criteria determine the time of their entrance or exit?*

In what ways are participants grouped? For instance, do students take part in the program *en masse* as members of classrooms or smaller subgroups? Is it most appropriate to talk about participants in terms of districts, buildings, classrooms, or individuals? How many participants per class or group?* Do program sites differ in significant ways (e.g., size, student body composition, administrative structure)? What differences in background, qualifications, or experience characterize the program participants?*

F. Budget and Administrative Arrangements

What period of time is covered by these funds? What has been the total cost of implementing this program?* What are the major cost items? What is the per pupil cost of the program?* What formula has been used for computing this figure?[2] How does the per pupil cost of the program compare with per pupil cost at the various sites where the program did not exist?*

From what sources have program funds been obtained? What proportion of program costs are paid by the system, by grants from the federal or state government, or by foundations?* Was the program developed with a specific funding source in mind? What proportion of program costs consists of monies that would have been spent anyway?* What proportion of monies is made up of funds specifically granted for operating the program?* If the program has run for several years or several funding periods, what changes in funding source and cost trends have occurred?

Of the cost of the program, what portion in rough dollar estimates could be called start-up and what portion could be called continuation costs?[3]

Depending upon the figures you have available to you, what breakdown by broad categories and amounts can you show of the total cost of the program?* For example, what are the costs of acquiring, maintaining, and operating the program plan? What has been the cost of developing materials? How much is it costing to disseminate information about the program? What were the salaries of various personnel categories?

Where can the reader obtain more detailed budget information?

How is the program administered? What offices or roles have been created or expanded? Does this represent a departure from the usual practice? Are the administrative arrangements that have been made major components of the program themselves, or does administration merely support a program whose main focus is instructional?

Questions About Program Specifics

A. Planned Program Characteristics

If a program plan has directed the implementation study, what does it say the program is *supposed* to look like? How highly prescribed is the program implementation? How much is the program allowed to vary from site to site or from time to time? What evidence is there that the program that has been implemented resembles the one the planners intended?

If a theory, philosophical stance, model for schooling, or expert opinion has directed the implementation, what program features does this orientation require you to examine? Why?

Does the plan or theory underlying your implementation study stipulate that something it considers detrimental be *absent* from the program? What and why?

Has the program been implemented at every site as planned and as the audience expected? If not, what happened? Have some components been dropped or modified? Are all materials available? Have they been used? Has the program been delivered to the audience for whom it was planned? Have crucial activities in fact occurred?

What provisions does the program establish for periodic review? How often should it occur? Are reviews done internally or do they include outside assistance? What techniques are used to monitor or modify program operations on a day-to-day basis? What reports must be submitted and to whom?

What planning or problem-solving meetings occur to help remedy program problems or to share program successes? What decisions are made on the basis of review or information on program weaknesses or strengths?

B. Program Materials and Facilities

For *each set of materials* your evaluation examines, answer the following questions:

Do the materials seem to fit the program's goals and objectives?*

What materials does the program actually use and how?* Which have been most often used? Seldom used? Never used?* Which were purchased and which were produced in-house?

Are the materials generally durable or must they be replaced fairly often (e.g., more than once every two years)? What percentage of the total materials purchased must be replaced?* How often?*

If *special materials* have been developed or adapted for the program, who did this, and when (e.g., over the summer, after school)? Were program funds provided?

   If readers want to obtain or duplicate these materials, from what source are they available?

   If materials have been custom-produced, have developers provided the quantity needed in the time allotted and with the funds available?

   Where and how could someone examine a complete set of the materials developed in-house?

If *commercially produced materials* have been purchased, which ones, how many, and at what cost?* For what grade level or for what groups?*

   What selection procedure was used?

   Were the materials ordered and delivered in sufficient time to allow their meaningful use?

   Where and how could someone examine a complete set of the purchased materials? Are they available for inspection in the school or district or only from the publisher or developer?

What evaluation procedures has the program established for reviewing the effectiveness of different materials?

What degree of structure, sequencing, and adaptation to the needs of individual participants is evident in the materials?*

What evidence is there that instructors and students found the materials interesting, stimulating, or useful?*

What other resources (e.g., physical facilities, transportation) have been used to support the program, and who provided them? For example, are special facilities provided by community groups? Is district transportation available for field trips?

Have any program settings outside the classroom been used (e.g., playground, special classroom, gym, field trip locale)? What percentage of program time was spent at each place?* What was the effect of the different settings?*

C. Program Activities

For *each different activity* that the program has encompassed, consider the following questions:

How do the activities fit the program's stated goals and objectives?

In what activities have participants in the program taken part? To what extent (often, fairly often, seldom, never)?* Which staff members direct the activities?

How much variation has there been in the program from site to site and from time to time?* How much of this variation was planned and how much was unexpected?

What measures have program staff taken to motivate students to participate in activities?* Were these methods planned in advance? Do they seem to work?*

What do the critical activities that make up the program look like in practice?* Are sources of information available (e.g., informal comments, narrative summaries, photographs, sketches, parent letters, student products) that you can copy or quote to support the findings indicated by your data? Were testimonials about the program that you have collected solicited or voluntary?

What evidence is there that program activities are interesting and valuable to students and teachers?

How are students grouped for various program activities?* How much interpersonal instructional contact do the activities give to students?* Does this vary greatly according to student characteristics? What are the teacher-pupil (or other role) ratios during the various program activities?

What is included in a typical day's or week's schedule of activity for the program participants?* How much time is devoted to various activities? What time of day do these occur? In what sequence do participants experience them?

What specific routine procedures, if any, do teachers or other program implementers follow?* How are these procedures communicated to students?

What amount and kinds of practice, review, and quizzes are provided for students in the program?* What are the content, frequency, and methods used in such activities?

Does a comparison or control group exist for the purpose of your implementation evaluation? If yes:

> What does the comparison group look like? How does the comparison group compare to the program group on important variables, particularly those that relate to program selection (e.g., age, grade levels, previous experience)?* What characteristics of the control participants can be pointed out to show that they are essentially the *same* as the program participants? What characteristics make them *different* from program participants?*

> Are comparison group students grouped in the same ways as program students?

> What are the important differences in the activities of the comparison group and the activities of the program group? Which materials, personnel, and facilities used by the comparison group are similar to those in the program?* Which are different?

> If the comparison group is a non-randomized, non-equivalent one, can you confidently make the following statement: "Although students were not randomly assigned to the control and program groups, our data show them to be so alike in critical features related to the program that they might as well have been randomly distributed to groups"? Why or why not?

> How does the rate of dropout and influx of the comparison group compare with that of the program group?* How do these rates compare with the dropout and influx rate typical of the comparison group's own school or district?

How do participants receive feedback about their individual progress (e.g., through verbal or written critiques of their work, regular classroom quizzes)?*

How are parents or supervisors informed about their students' progress?* For example, have parent-teacher conferences been held? How frequently?* Have parents been invited to observe their children in class?* To what extent has parental advice been sought in planning individual children's activities?*

If problems with parents or the community have affected the program, what steps, if any, have been taken to remedy them?

Do program participants feel that the program as it currently exists could be improved if it were modified or run for a longer period of time? Is there evidence in your data to support their point of view? What conclusions about extent or quality of program implementation have you been able to draw from your examination of program activities?

Questions About the Evaluation Itself

A. Purpose and Focus of the Evaluation

Is this evaluation primarily formative or summative? That is, will your information feed back to the staff for the purpose of program improvement, or will the implementation study constitute a program summary?

Who are the audiences for the report? The program staff? Parents or supervisors? Community? School board? State or federal agencies?

Is the implementation study being undertaken to assess the match between the program as implemented and the program as planned? To examine the implementation of a theory or point of view? Will the evaluation use qualitative methods to describe what is happening in the program regardless of what was formally planned?

What period of time is covered by the report? How much of the entire program does it cover?

What is the context of the implementation study? Are there restrictions, constraints of time or money, or other limitations influencing the course and direction of your study? Are there particular issues that you have decided not to address? Did you make this decision alone or in consultation with the program staff ?

Which critical program characteristics—materials and activities—have you chosen to concentrate on in gathering your data? Why? Were activities selected because of their sheer critical weight to the program? If so, how was critical weight determined?

If you are not attempting to compare actual with planned program occurrence, how did you decide which activities or materials to describe? Alone or in consultation with program staff or others?

Is your selection of program features to examine representative of the total program? What provisions have you made to detect or allow for program variations across sites or over time?

For which aspects of your evaluation have you decided to collect supporting data? Why? For which aspects *might* you have chosen to collect such data but did not? Why?

What questions are program staff most interested in answering? What information will best answer these questions? Will your plan for data collection gather sufficient information for you to answer these questions?

What formal report requirements, if any, are there? What types of reports would be most useful to program staff? Will program participants be informed of the evaluation's results? If appropriate, how will the community be informed about your findings?

B. Implementing Measures and Data Collection Procedures

What types of instruments have you chosen to use as your sources of data? Will you rely on informal information gathering methods (e.g., casual observations or conversations with program staff) or formal methods (e.g., systematic observation or questionnaires)? Are you using some combination of these types? Why?

How have instruments been selected? Have you found ready-made ones to copy or purchase? From whom and on what basis?

If instruments have been developed, who undertook the task? What were their time and budget constraints? What are their qualifications for developing measures?* How did they go about developing the measures?

What limitations or deficiencies are there in the instruments used?

Were checks made on instrument validity, reliability, and appropriateness to the setting?*

What data collection procedures were used? What was the schedule for the collection of implementation information? Who collected it?

What training was provided and what precautions taken to ensure appropriate use of instruments?*

Were instruments (e.g., questionnaires, interview schedules) administered to everyone or to a representative group? Who? How were they chosen, or, in other words, what sampling plan did you use?

What limitations or deficiencies were there in the sampling or scheduling used for measuring implementation?

Summary

Preparing an effective implementation report requires that you consider many different questions, some relating to the program in general, some to specific elements of the program, and some to features of the evaluation itself. The preceding list includes a variety of questions for your consideration, and, in summary, it may be helpful to ask three additional questions:

— Do you eventually have to include all the information you collect as a result of these questions in some sort of report?
— Will every evaluation address every question given on the preceding pages?
— Does this list include every possible question an implementation evaluation could consider?

The answer to all three questions is "Of course not." The purpose of the list is merely to help you generate ideas that may make your evaluation more useful. To the extent that you can understand key program concerns and issues and gain a sense of what can be done to improve the program, your evaluation will focus on areas of use to program staff and participants. However, a list such as this cannot hope to include all questions critical to specific evaluation contexts. It is likely, though, that if you have thought about each of the questions carefully in light of the program you are evaluating, you will have brought to the surface important issues that will help you frame a good study.

Notes

1. Needs assessment is a process by which the *goals* of an organization, such as a school, are first selected or generated and then assigned priorities. This process, which seeks to determine the needs of the organization, usually asks members of its constituency—say, the community or the parent agency—to express opinions.
2. A start-up cost is money and time spent on *development* of a program, for example, planning, materials, and facilities—things that occur only once in the life of the program.

Continuation costs are expenditures needed to keep the program running once it is off the ground. For example, continuation costs are reflected in the annual salaries of the teachers hired especially for the program.

3. A useful figure for describing cost per pupil results from dividing all costs paid out of program funds by the number of pupils who attended the program on what you have defined as a regular basis. This number eliminates excessive absentees from the total number of students. You might also calculate a per pupil cost based only on continuation costs. In order to do this, subtract the start-up costs from the total program expenditure before dividing by the number of participants.

Index

NOTES